The Better Money Method

Terry Laxton

The Better Money Method
A Better Idea for Retirement

Poor-on-Paper Press
Seattle, Washington

Poor-on-Paper Press
Seattle, Washington
www.bettermoneymethod.com

Printed in the United States of America

ISBN: 978-0-692-01102-7

This book is dedicated to Christine, my wife and the love of my life, who has been my best friend ever since I was nineteen and an extraordinary mother to our three wonderful children. Without her love and constant support, I would not be the person I am today.

All truth goes through three stages: It is ridiculed; then it is radically opposed; and only much later will it be accepted as self-evident.

—Arthur Schopenhauer

Contents

Acknowledgments

I would like to thank my editor, Paul Weisser, for all his dedication to the production of this book. Paul's professionalism and commitment to clarity and honesty have helped me enormously. His constant prodding for clarification forced me to dig deep, and the result has been a much better book than I ever could have written without his assistance and guidance.

I would also like to thank Jenean Cameron for all her efforts on the great illustrations in this book.

About the Author:
A Constructive Maverick

We're all mad here. I'm mad. You're mad.
— The Cat in *Alice in Wonderland*

When I was a little kid, my mother always told me to wear clean underwear because, she said, if I ever got in an accident, *they* would find out that my underpants were soiled. I always wondered who *they* were, and never much liked them.

As I grew older, there were always a lot of *theys* in my way, but I never much cared what they thought. At 21, when I was straight out of college and in my first job, as an elementary school teacher of fifth-graders, the *they* were my school principal. What happened was that I immediately realized that all the kids in my class were way below grade level in math—so I went to the other three fifth-grade teachers to ask why, and their answer stunned me. The series of math books that the school used, they said, had been purchased when my kids were first-graders, and it wasn't time to buy a new series until next year. So even though the current series was totally ineffective—in fact, destructive—the school was going to have to stay with it for another year. And no one questioned that.

The math "book" was actually a collection of five "comic

books," each one on a different aspect of math. I decided that the books were in the totally wrong order, so at the Christmas break, I had the kids turn in all their copies, and then I cut them up and put them back together into one volume that made more sense to me. When the kids got back from vacation, they weren't at all fazed by what I had done. They were probably even pleased by what they perceived as my "mischief." They certainly knew I was different from the other teachers, and they expected me to do "crazy" things from time to time.

About two months later, the school principal came to see me when he learned that my kids were outperforming all the other fifth-graders in math, and he was curious to find out what I was doing to get that result. However, when I showed him the cut-up books, he was furious that I had destroyed school property. After that incident, when it was clear to me that the system was more interested in its self-preservation and maintaining the bureaucratic status quo than in the kids' academic progress, I knew I was in the wrong profession.

For the previous several years, I had been fascinated by how homes get built and properties developed, so on my weekends I had often visited building sites to see what was going on. Originally, I hadn't thought of this as a profession but only as a hobby. But when I contemplated quitting teaching, I figured I might become a self-employed independent home builder and property developer. That would free me, I thought, from the bureaucratic *they*, put me in charge of my own destiny, and give me the opportunity to make as much money as I could. For the next twenty years, that's precisely what I did—loving the feeling of being responsible for building all the houses in a neighborhood.

My grandfather had been a builder and property developer before I was even born, so perhaps my interest ran in my genes. In any case, he told me that, in his day, he could buy a piece of property, hire his engineers, design a subdivision, and all he needed to do after that was go down to city hall and sit down around a pot of coffee with the city engineers. They would tell him to put in a fire hydrant here or resize a water line there—and four hours later, he and his crew would start building.

Originally, that was more or less how I operated, too. If I wanted to build a small subdivision, all I had to do was design it, go down to city hall with my plans on a sheet of paper, pay a $20 permit fee, and start building that very day. But over a period of time, the local and state bureaucrats started to get more intrusive, and eventually, to build that same subdivision, I would have to pay consultants $100,000 to do their studies and calculations, and it could take a year and a half or two to get the city's permission to build. So, once again, *they* had found me.

After I had been "retired" for a couple of years, my wife said to me one day, "You probably oughta get your butt out of the house once in a while." As a builder and developer, I had been sitting across from bankers for years, and believed I could do as good a job as any of them, so I became a mortgage broker. Once again, I figured, I could free myself from the bureaucratic *they* and be in charge of my own destiny.

It didn't take long for me to make a shocking discovery that really opened my eyes. Mortgage brokers are about the only folks who get to see people's whole financial picture, and I learned that 95% of Americans reach retirement age without the means to maintain their lifestyle, with very little liquidity and almost no savings.* All that, I discovered, resulted from the introduction in the 1970s of IRAs, 401(k)s, 403(b)s, and so on. In effect, those retirement plans ask "amateurs" to be their own pension fund managers. But most folks know very little about money management, so when they plan for their retirement, they don't know how much to invest, how to

*Sharon A. DeVaney and Sophia T. Chiremba, *Comparing the Retirement Savings of the Baby Boomers and Other Cohorts* (March 16, 2005), retrieved on September 25, 2009, from http://www.bls.gov/opub/cwc/cm20050114ar01p1.htm/

minimize their risk, and how to maximize their rate of return.

In the beginning, I didn't know, either. So, for two years, I read every book on financial planning I could get my hands on, and I attended every seminar that promised to have a shred of enlightenment on the subject. With my ingrained contempt for *they*, I didn't start out with any preconceptions, but had a totally open mind to anything that made sense. It quickly became apparent to me, however, that a lot of people believed in a lot of things that weren't true. As Will Rogers once said, "The problem in America isn't so much what people don't know; the problem is what people think they know that just ain't so."

In other words, if you keep doing what everybody else is doing, you're gonna get what everyone else is getting. I concluded that if 95% of Americans were not getting security and peace of mind when they retired, I didn't have to be a rocket scientist to figure out that the system wasn't working. There *had* to be a better way. Until I learned some answers, I was making the same mistakes as everybody else — going over the cliff as fast as any other lemming.

What really shocked me was that it wasn't only Mr. and Mrs. America who didn't know how to manage money for the long term. The so-called professional "experts" didn't know any more than they did. For starters, they didn't have the most basic knowledge of what the best tools are for achieving a secure retirement. These "experts" included financial planners, stockbrokers, insurance agents, and investment "guru" celebrities of every stripe. They had "information" alright, but it was filled with half-truths — when it wasn't outright false.

Traditionally, investment advisors have dealt with the risks in the stock market by urging their clients to diversify their assets and stay in for the long haul. However, those strategies didn't protect you in the market meltdown of 2001–2003. And if you waited for the market to come back, it took you till 2007 to break even. But if you got your shirt back from *that* meltdown, the one in 2008 not only took your shirt back but grabbed your underwear, too!

For example, if you invested $100,000 in the S&P 500 in 1999, when the market was red hot, at the end of 2008 your investment would have been worth only $75,000. On the other hand, if you had followed the advice in this book, your investment at the end of 2008 would have been worth $175,000! So, which way would *you* like to go?

What if you could take the gambling out of investing? You already insure your car and probably your house against potential risks. Why not your investments, too? My advice for avoiding risk is simple: *Don't lose money and don't be greedy.*

But how do you not lose money? Most people think they have to accept risk as part of making a decent rate of return. In fact, that's totally untrue and even counterproductive. Think about this: If you had enough money to buy a major league baseball team and had two choices, which would you pick: (a) the team that had one superstar who hit a lot of homers, but everyone else was below average; or (b) the team that didn't have any superstars, but everyone consistently hit singles and doubles? By the end of the season, which team do you think would have won more games? The answer is obvious, and the same lesson applies to financial planning. The trouble is that when it comes to stocks, bonds, and real estate, most people are looking for the home-run king and ignoring the less glamorous steady hitters.

If you learn to minimize your risks, your interest expenses, your exposure to market loss, and your taxes, you will achieve four things:

- *a higher rate of return*
- *a secure retirement*
- *a more comfortable lifestyle*
- *peace of mind*

How to achieve all these things is what I learned in my unbiased search for truth, and I feel obligated now to share my findings with the general public. My discoveries were so amazing that people often think at first that they are too good to be true. But the solutions, which I call the Better Money Method,™ are both true and straightforward. All you will need to do is have an open mind and *use* it.

Terry Laxton
Investment Advisor Representative

Chapter 1:

The Story of Ted and Alice Goode

This story is drawn from real-life examples and applies to everyone—doctors, lawyers, truck drivers, teachers, plumbers, rich or middle-class. The only difference for YOU is how many zeroes you put on the end of the numbers.

Ted Goode and his cousin Bob Bedderoff took two different paths forward to their retirement. In this chapter, we will look at Ted, who took a traditional approach to investing, along with his wife, Alice. In the following chapters, we will look at Bob, who started off in the same place financially as Ted, but took the Better Money Method™ path to investing, and wound up with *millions* of dollars more for himself and his wife, Becky.

When Ted graduated from college, he went to work for a well-known Seattle-based airplane company for a starting annual salary of $35,000. Since he was an engineer, he was into numbers and had always appreciated the time value of money. In other words, he knew that the earlier he started investing, the less money he would have to put in at the beginning to end up at the same place—or the more he would have because he started younger.

For example, if Ted started, at the age of twenty-two, putting

$300 a month ($3,600 a year) into his retirement account, earning compound interest at 8%, by age sixty-five (that is, 43 years later) that account, which amounted to his investing $154,800, would be worth $1,342,483.

On the other hand, if he waited until he was thirty-two to put in the same $300 a month, that would amount to an investment in 33 years of $118,800, which at 8% compound interest would be worth $580,094. So, the ten years during which he failed to invest, which are less than a quarter of 43 years, would cost him 57% of his final balance! To end up with the same $1,342,483 after 33 years, he would have had to make monthly payments more than twice as big as what was required in 43 years—namely, $694 a month ($8,328 a year), instead of $300 a month ($3,600 year).

With these numbers in hand, Ted was eager to sign up for his company's 401(k) plan, the sooner the better. When he went down to see Helen Wheels, the Human Resources representative, she gave him three reasons why the 401(k) option was such a good idea.

"First of all, Ted," she said, "the company will match your contributions, up to $1,500 per year."

"That sounds like free money to me…. I like *that*."

"Everybody does, Ted. Furthermore, the 401(k) will be the best place to save money for your future, because your contributions will be tax-deferred. So, if you put $1,500 a year into your 401(k), and the company throws in another $1,500, you'll only have to pay taxes on $33,500 in income…, rather than the $35,000 you're actually earning. In fact, with the company's contribution, you're really getting $36,500 a year, but paying taxes on $33,500."

"I like the idea of lower taxes," Ted said, "but how does tax deferral actually work? I'm not sure I quite understand it."

"It's not all that complicated, Ted. You'll be in a lower tax bracket when you retire, since your income will go down…, so, naturally, you'll pay lower taxes on your income during your retirement years."

"That makes sense. Let me think about it."

"Think all you like. It's a terrific deal," Helen said.

As a good engineer, Ted didn't take anything for granted, so he decided to get a second opinion. The first thing he did was visit his accountant, Molly Muddles, to see what she thought of 401(k)s.

"I think they're a great deal," Molly said, "because you'll get a tax deduction during the years you put money into your plan, and that money will grow and compound without being taxed until you retire. At that point, taxes will kick in, but you'll be in a lower tax bracket than when you were working, just as your HR rep said."

That all sounded wonderful, but Ted still wanted to check it out further. So, he went to get the advice of an old family friend, George Phollows. Like Ted, George was an engineer, and he had worked his way up into senior management in the same airplane manufacturing company that Ted worked in, so, late one afternoon, Ted stopped by his office.

"I totally agree with Helen and your accountant," George said. "401(k)s are definitely the way to go. Like they said, you'll get a tax deduction every year you put money in…, you'll get the company's matching funds, which really *are* free money, as you said…, and you'll be in a lower tax bracket when you retire. What's not to like? I've got one myself."

"You don't see any downside to 401(k)s, George?"

"Absolutely not. They're totally safe. Just look at all the other investments I've made and where *they* landed me. One time, I got into a limited partnership with some friends to develop a piece of property. They all assured me, with the real estate market hot the way it was, there was *no* way we could miss making a fortune. But then the county got in on the act, with all the bureaucratic red tape they're so good at, and when they were finished with us, the project came on line two years later than we had figured. Guess what happened next? We were ready just as the real estate market was tanking. To get out of the deal, we had to sell the lots at a loss. 401(k)s sure beat the hell out of that, don't they, Ted?"

"I can't argue with you there."

"Then there was the time I got a so-called 'hot tip' from another friend, who had just bought some sexy new tech stock. But right after I bought it, I found out, the hard way, that I was the last one to get the tip. The stock had already capped out! And I could tell you more 'war stories' about my investments. I could probably go on for hours. The bottom line, Ted, is go with the 401(k)s. You'll never be sorry."

Based on all this advice, Ted rushed over to see Helen, and signed up for his 401(k) on the spot.

Five years later, Ted was married to Alice, and they had three children, whom they loved very much and were very proud of: Jennifer, or "Jenny," age 4; Addie, age 2; and Ted, Jr., or "Teddy," who was a month old. During those five years, Ted was an excellent employee, working long hours, and his income steadily increased accordingly. In fact, he and Alice were able to increase Ted's annual contribution to his 401(k) plan to $5,000 per year from his initial $1,500 contribution. The company's annual contribution, however, remained at $1,500.

Unfortunately, the following year, while taking the kids to the park one day, Alice had a car accident. The good news was that she and the kids were not hurt. All the other news was bad. To begin with, the police decided that the accident was totally Alice's fault. Furthermore, Ted and Alice's auto insurance policy was not as comprehensive as they had thought. Ted had done his homework when he bought the policy, so he figured he was covered for this accident. In fact, he and Alice had both agreed that minimum insurance levels required by their state were too low—$20,000 per individual, $50,000 total personal injury per accident, and $10,000 for property damage—so they had voluntarily increased their insurance to $100,000 per person, $300,000 total personal injury per accident, and $50,000 for property damage. Therefore, until now, they had never given the policy much thought. However, they soon found out that, even with the increases they had made, they had a serious problem.

First of all, of the three people in the other car, one had to go to the hospital with severe injuries. In the end, she had to have multiple reconstructive surgeries and six months of physical therapy, which cost a total of $136,000. In addition to that, she was unable to work for six months, which cost an additional $35,000 in lost wages.

"Goodness, Ted!" Alice said, looking really sad. "Our policy has a limit of $100,000 per person. That means we have to come up with the other $71,000 out of our own pockets."

"*Mama mia!*" Ted said. "$71,000! Where are we going to get our hands on *that* kind of money?"

"Can we borrow it from your credit union?"

"I guess so. And pay it back over five years with interest."

The next afternoon, Alice got a call from her insurance agent.

"I've got some bad news, Alice," he began. "You had the misfortune of hitting a high-end Mercedes, and they cost a helluva lot of money to fix. Are you sitting down?"

"Oh, my! That bad, huh?"

"I'm afraid so. The repairs on that baby came to $54,000. Since your policy only covers $50,000 in property damage, that leaves over only $4,000 to pay out of pocket."

"Darn!" Alice said. "And in addition to that, we still owe $50,000 on the Suburban. I really did it this time."

Not wanting to depress Ted while he was at work, Alice saved this news for after dinner that evening, when the kids were asleep.

"There's no way out, Ted," she said at the end of her story. "I'm going to have to take a job for a while. I hate to have to put the kids in day care, but I can't see how else we're going to be able to make payments on a new car while paying off all our other debts."

"I can't see any other way, either, honey," Ted said. "I guess we're going to have to stop funding the 401(k) for a few years."

"Does that mean losing the matching funds, too?"

"I'm afraid it does. Darn it, we have no choice.... But don't worry, we'll get through it somehow."

It took them four years to get "through it," but they made it. Thanks to Ted's raises at work, they paid off the $75,000 debt (actually, with interest, over $80,000) a year ahead of schedule.

"You know what, Alice?" Ted said one day. "We need to make up for that lost time by increasing our 401(k) contributions to $15,000 a year..., which is the maximum the law allows us right now."

"That'll be a bit of a strain for us, Ted, but we do want a comfortable retirement."

"The trouble is, honey, how do we get that and put away some funds at the same time for the kids' college years? I just don't see how we can do both."

"We'll find a way, Ted. You'll see. You keep getting raises, and I still have my job at Starbucks."

The trouble was that, two years after Ted and Alice were able to resume funding Ted's 401(k), Alice's father had a heart attack and needed some financial assistance. Since Alice's mother had died five years before, and Alice had no siblings, she was the only one who could help her father in this time of need.

"You know how important Dad is to me, Ted. We have to find a way to give him the money he needs..., about $15,000. But since we're max-funding the 401(k), trying to make up for that lost time, I know we don't have much in the way of liquid reserves. And the credit union has a freeze on loans at the moment because of the current economic situation."

"There's one more option, Alice," Ted said, "although I never thought it would come to this.... I can take a loan out against my 401(k)."

"Oh, Ted, I don't like it…. But I think that's what we have to do."

The next day, when Ted went to HR to find out what the process was for taking out such a loan, Helen Wheels had some unpleasant news for him.

"Yeah, you can do it, Ted," she said. "But there are strings attached."

"Doesn't anything in life come without strings?"

"Not much…. In this case, you'll have to sell some of the mutual fund stock in your 401(k) to create the cash. That will reduce the amount of money in the account, which means that it will not grow as fast. The second string is that you'll have to repay the money in five years or less."

"What happens if I don't? For example, what happens if I get laid off?"

"In that case, or if you had to quit work for *any* reason, you'll have to repay the loan within ninety days."

"And if I can't do *that?*"

"If you can't do that, the government kicks you while you're down. You'll have to pay taxes on the loan as ordinary income and a ten percent penalty for an early withdrawal."

"This is all new to me," Ted said with irritation. "I was under the impression that the money in the 401(k) was mine. No one ever told me about all these damn strings!"

Nevertheless, the fact was that Ted really didn't have any alternatives, so he took the loan.

When he got home, he told Alice that they would have to repay the loan in five years or less. "I'm really worried," he said, "about the tax consequences if I should ever be laid off. I never had to worry about that before, but now it really bothers me, having a tax time bomb over our heads."

"Couldn't you stop your monthly contributions to the 401(k) for a while?" Alice asked. "Then you could use *that* money to repay the loan."

"I could," he said, "but then I would lose the company's matching funds again. What would be better is if I *reduced* my monthly contributions down to…let me get out my calculator…down to $833 from the $1,250 I put in now. That would be a drop from $15,000 a year to roughly $10,000, and if I use that $5,000 difference to pay off the loan, we'll be back on track in three years."

Five years later, Ted was earning $150,000 per year. Aside from the fact that Alice's father died two years ago, the couple had been enjoying a good life, especially since they paid off the 401(k) loan and Ted resumed making his annual $15,000 contributions to his 401(k) plan.

However, the time soon arrived for Jennifer to start college.

"Holy cow!" Alice said, dumbfounded as she put down a catalogue from one of the colleges Jennifer was applying to. "How did the cost of going to college get so high since our day, Ted? When you and I went to school, it cost about $10,000 a year. It says here in this catalogue that it's now closer to $40,000!"

Ted was stunned. "How in the world can anyone send their kids to college at that rate?"

The problem was that, although Ted had received nice annual raises, averaging about 4%, the cost of college during the same period had gone up an average of 7%.

The couple made every effort to find financial aid for Jennifer, but discovered that they had two strikes against them.

"First of all," a counselor at one of the colleges explained to them, "your income is too high, Mister Goode, to qualify Jenny for financial aid. Second, you have more than half a million dollars in equity in your home, and the college looks at home equity as liquid…, so I advise you to take out a new loan on your house to pay for Jenny's education."

Ted and Alice didn't like that idea very much. During the drive home, Alice said, "I guess, if you and I stopped going out to nice restaurants and gave up our family vacations, we'd be able to help Jenny get through college. Of course, she'll also have to work part-time and during the summers."

"I hate giving up our date nights," Ted said.

"I know, honey, I hate it, too. But Jenny has to come first."

"What are we gonna do, Alice, when it's time for Addie to start college in two years?"

"I know. And Teddy isn't far behind!"

After much thought, Ted said to Alice, "I think our best course of action would be to tough it out the first two years that Jenny's in college…, give up the date nights, the vacations, and all that. Plus, she gets a job. Two years from now, we'll have to take out a new mortgage to help Addie."

"It's not the most appealing idea I've ever heard from you, Ted Goode," Alice said, "but we want our kids to get a college education, and I can't think of any other solution."

"Neither can I, honey. At least, Jenny will be getting out of college a year before Teddy starts, so we won't have to pay for all three of them in school at the same time."

A few years later, when Ted turned 59, he and Alice were happy that they had been able to help their children finish college and get good jobs. It had been a struggle, but well worth it. For the last few years, they had been able to go out to fine restaurants again and to enjoy some of the other good things in life. For the last eight years, they had also been able to max-fund Ted's 401(k) plan, so they now have just under a million dollars in it, which made them feel pretty good.

Unfortunately, they now had a new concern. When the government put in a universal health-care plan, a few years back, the cost of that, combined with the costs of Medicare, Medicaid, and other government programs, drove the federal tax rate up to 49%.

I never thought I'd live to see this day," Ted said. "And when you add in the state income tax, we've got less than half of our income for ourselves. That sure gives new meaning to *deferred taxes*. When I first started out, they told me that my taxes would be lower when I retired. That was the whole point of getting the 401(k) in the first place…, that and the matching funds. Now I see that the only way my taxes could be lower today than they were then is if I hadn't been so successful in saving!"

"Isn't that amazing?" Alice said. "We'd have to be poor now for our taxes to go down."

"Yeah, for the lousy few thousand dollars in taxes that we supposedly 'saved' by putting money into my 401(k), we now get the 'privilege' of higher taxes on *all* the money when we pull it out. And there's no guarantee that taxes won't go even higher by the time I retire."

Just before Ted turned 59^1/$_2$, he went to his company's HR department to tell them that he wanted to withdraw all of his 401(k) funds to invest them himself.

Helen Wheels was retired by now, and living frugally in Florida, so Ted had to present his request to the new HR rep, Les Witz.

"My wife and I," Ted began, "know that the tax code allows me to take money out of my 401(k) without any penalty, starting a month from now, when I turn fifty-nine and a half. We've decided to take advantage of that. What we want to do is take all the money out of the plan, pay the current taxes on it, and then get the money working for us in tax-free investments, like municipal bonds."

Les frowned. "I'm so sorry, Ted," he said. "The government allows you to do all that, but the company doesn't."

"What?! What do you mean?"

"Under the provisions of your plan, you can't withdraw *any* money…, not a penny…, so long as you're an employee of this company. If you want to go ahead with your investment plans, the only way you can close out your 401(k) here is to quit your job."

"Quit my job?!"

"That's right."

"Where would I ever find a high-paying job like this at *my* age?"

"I hate to tell you this, Ted, but that's why some folks call these plans 'golden handcuffs.'"

"Why didn't someone tell me this thirty-five years ago?"

"Ted, thirty-five years ago, I was in kindergarten."

When Ted got home, totally demoralized, Alice said, "What's wrong? You look like a ghost."

"We're trapped, honey. Totally and completely trapped."

When he explained to her what the HR rep had told him, Alice said, "Why don't you talk to some of your friends at other companies. Maybe one of them will know a way to get out of this."

So, Ted called around, and found out that most of his friends' 401(k) plans had similar clauses. In fact, one of his friends didn't know it, either, so Ted's question ultimately caused him to be depressed, too.

Sitting around the kitchen table, with his head in his hands, Ted said to Alice, "I'm completely disillusioned with the whole concept of 401(k)s. They're a scam from top to bottom. And now that I know it, it's too late for me to do anything about it. I *hate* it that my money, which I worked so hard for all these years, is controlled by other people. And that baloney about my taxes going down after I retire…, with us in the 49% bracket now, what a lie! Somebody should go to jail for it!"

So, Ted kept working for the company and left his money in his 401(k) plan.

"Luckily for us," he said to Alice one evening, "the government's just raised the limits on contributions to 401(k)s. That means we'll be able to put in $25,000 every year from now on."

"That's good news, for a change, honey."

"Well, I've got a little *more* good news for you…. I was talking to Jeff and Harry this morning, and they told me their companies recently dropped their matching fund programs. At least, we've still got *that*."

One of the things that Ted and Alice had always wanted to do was buy a motor home and travel the country. For the last two years before Ted retired, they planned their itinerary, carefully studying road maps, reading books about various attractions, and making a list of places to visit and the best times of year to go there.

"I've always wanted to see Mount Rushmore," Alice said.

"And I can't wait to visit Gettysburg," said Ted, who was a Civil War buff.

By the time Ted retired at 65, and he and Alice were ready to set off, their federal taxes were at 50%, and their state taxes were at 15%. On the other hand, they still got a little money from Social Security, and the stock market had been good to them. Despite all their setbacks, they had managed to pay off their mortgage, and Ted's 401(k) had grown to just under $2 million. It looked as if the couple were going to do just fine in retirement.

"We'll have to buy a somewhat smaller motor home than we

originally planned," Ted said, "so we can conserve our cash."

"We don't need a rolling mansion," Alice said. "A modest one will do just fine. In fact, it'll bring us a little closer together."

They were thrilled on the day when they finally set out on the open road. Their kids were delighted to get postcards from Yellowstone National Park, Mount Rushmore, the Grand Canyon, the Alamo, and other attractions all over the country. Eight months into their trip, they had seen twenty states and were still having a great time.

One morning, when Alice got up, she noticed that Ted looked pale as he read that day's *Wall Street Journal*.

"What's wrong, Ted?" she said, almost afraid to ask. "Has someone died?"

"No, it's nothing like that.... The stock market dropped twenty percent yesterday. If it stays like that, our two million dollars will be down to about one and a half."

"What kind of a system *is* this," she said, "that allows people to work hard all their life, follow the rules, and still lose half their income after they retire?"

"It's not half yet, honey..., but if it keeps going like this, it will be soon."

Over breakfast, neither of them said a word. They were both too depressed. Alice was the one who finally broke the silence.

"Maybe," she said, "we should have been a little less aggressive with our portfolio.... Fewer stocks and more bonds."

"Yeah, hindsight is always twenty-twenty, Alice. But if you recall, we didn't think the return on bonds would cover our expenses."

"Well," she said, "talking about expenses, I've read that people shouldn't pull out more than four percent of their funds every year if they want to be sure that their money won't run out during their lifetime. At that rate, with our million and a half dollars, four percent would come to...."

"About sixty thousand dollars a year, Alice. I already figured it out."

"Goodness gracious, Ted! That's not going to get us very far."

"It sure isn't. And I don't want you living like a pauper when I'm gone, either. I guess I'm going to have to find some kind of part-time work somewhere."

So, they ended their trip, sold their motor home, Ted got a part-time job as a consultant, and they spent their remaining years living modestly. Ted worked as long as he could, and after that the couple bought a smaller house and later got a reverse mortgage to make ends meet. Ted lived to the ripe age of 91; and Alice, to 95. But the saddest part of their story was that they had spent most of their retirement years living in only a shadow of their former lifestyle— something neither of them had anticipated.

Furthermore, they had somehow managed to hide this fact from their children. By the time Alice passed away, the couple's nest egg had shrunk down to half a million dollars—and would have been even smaller if they hadn't reduced their lifestyle down to the bare essentials. But because of the overspending by the government, the estate tax exemption had long ago been eliminated. The federal tax rate was now up to 56 percent, and the state tax rate was at 18 percent. Worse yet, because Alice had not set up a trust and transferred her assets into it, her estate had to be probated, which meant that, by law, an attorney got paid 6 percent. That left 20 percent for the kids: $100,000 divided by three, or $33,333.33 each—with an extra penny for Jenny as the oldest.

When they thought about how hard their parents had worked all their lives to save their money, Jenny, Addie, and Teddy were furious.

"What really ticks me off," Addie said, "is how Mom and Dad cut back their expenses so sharply just so they wouldn't run out of money."

"Yeah," Jenny agreed. "And in the end, they leave half a million bucks behind, which they should have spent on themselves..., and now the government comes along and grabs most of it."

"It makes me sick," Teddy said. "There just *has* to be a better way.... But I'll be darned if I know what it is."

Chapter 2:
The Story of Bob Bedderoff

When Bob Bedderoff graduated from law school, he joined a law firm in Denver at a starting annual salary of $40,000. Like his cousin Ted, he spoke to the representative at the Human Resources Department of his firm about his retirement, but somehow he just didn't like the concept of 401(k)s. Being an attorney, he was used to reading the fine print in documents, and several aspects of the 401(k) plan disturbed him. He especially disliked the idea that he wouldn't be able to pull out his money unless and until he left his employer. Nevertheless, before making a decision, he decided to talk things over with his parents.

Essentially, Martin and Florence Bedderoff, Bob's parents, had had the same experience with Martin's 401(k) that we have just witnessed with Ted's. In fact, their situation was a little worse, because their health hadn't been nearly as good as Ted's and Alice's, and a good deal of their money had gone to doctors and hospitals.

"What frustrates us so much," Florence said to her son, "is that we did exactly what everyone told us to do. And although we did that to the best of our ability, it just hasn't seemed to work out, and we really don't know why."

"If you had it to do all over again," Bob asked his parents, "what would you do?"

Martin and Florence thought about that for a long time. Then Martin said, "You know, about ten years ago, your Uncle Justin was talking about some 'harebrained scheme' called the Better Money Method. At the time, when he described it to us, we thought he had just about lost his mind. He tried to get us to meet his investment advisor, but we thought it would be a waste of time, and never did it. Now Aunt Nicole tells us that she and Justin are getting ready to retire, and they've got a cash cow set up to keep them in comfort for the rest of their lives. You oughta give your Uncle Justin a call and see how he did it. I sure wish *we* had when we had the chance. Now it's too late for us..., but not for you."

Soon after he got home, Bob phoned his Uncle Justin.

"I'm glad you called," Justin said. "It sounds like your parents have finally gotten some sense. I've tried for years to get them to open their minds, but they're no different than most folks. When I tell people what I've been doing with my money, they either think I'm nuts or tell me it's too good to be true."

"*Is* it too good to be true, Uncle Justin? Tell me how it works."

"I'd be more than happy to tell you what Nicole and I have done, Bob. But, you know, a lot of people are afraid to take a different path than everyone else. So, if that's where you're coming from, I would just as soon not waste your time...or mine."

"No," Bob said, "I really want to educate myself about my options. I can't say for sure that I'll follow your advice until I learn more about it, but I can say I don't like what I've learned so far about 401(k)s and IRAs. It seems to me they have a lot of restrictions on them, and I want to control my own money, instead of letting the government call all the shots."

"You've got that right!"

"Yeah, well, I'm a young attorney without a whole lot of experience, but it sure looks like there are many ways to get cross-threaded on these plans. First of all, they're just based on laws, and laws can be changed any time Congress wants to. There are no guarantees the government won't change the ground rules in the future. From what

I've seen, that's exactly what it does. Secondly, employers can and usually do add additional restrictions to the 401(k) plans above and beyond the law. So, if there's a smarter way for me to have control over my own retirement funds, I'm all ears."

"Well, then, Bob, I'd be delighted to tell you more about the Better Money Method. The first thing you need to know about it is that it's a concept or system…, a combination of some very powerful tools into a method that has totally changed our lives. When your aunt and I were first introduced to the Method, ten years ago, we were on the same track as your parents. Your dad was fifty-one at the time, and I was fifty. Over the years, I had seen my 401(k) go up and down like a yo-yo. But all the advisors I talked to just kept telling me to remember that this was a long-term strategy. 'If you just stick with it,' they would say, 'you'll do fine in the long run.' But that just didn't wash with Nicole and me when we saw the balance in our 401(k) take ten years just to get back to where it had been. So, we had enough of all that excitement with the ups and downs of the market. We couldn't see a way to retire with any security under a system like that."

"Uncle Justin, that's exactly the same conclusion I was coming to."

"That's because you're a smart boy, Bob. Now, just around that time, ten years ago, a co-worker of mine told me about a seminar he had just gone to that he was very excited about. 'I suggest you and Nicole get yourself down there and see what it's all about,' he said. Well, we did, and what we heard was counter to everything we had ever been told before. At first, Nicole and I looked at each other as if the man was charming but a little off his rocker. But then he started to make a lot of sense when he asked a thought-provoking question. 'If you were a farmer,' he said, 'what would you rather do? Pay tax on the seed, and get the harvest tax-free, or get the seed tax-free and pay tax on the harvest?' Well, obviously, everyone wanted to pay tax on the seed."

"Of course, that makes perfect sense. The harvest is going to be worth a lot more than the seed, so the taxes on it would also be higher."

"Exactly. But then the man pointed out that with our IRAs and our 401(k)s, we're literally paying taxes on the harvest!"

"Ouch!"

"Ouch is right! That's when we sat up straight and paid close attention to everything else he said. First of all, he told us how IRAs and 401(k)s originated."

"I was wondering about that. Where *did* they come from?"

"That's a story all by itself, Bob. Basically, they began in the mid-1970s. But they were never meant back then to be used the way they are today. You know, most folks think of IRAs and 401(k)s as their primary retirement vehicle…, because that's what they've turned into. But when they were first introduced, they were only intended to be a supplement to traditional retirement plans, not a replacement for them."

"By traditional retirement plans, you mean company-sponsored plans, right?"

"Yeah, like your grandpa had. But over the years, more and more companies saw 401(k)s as a way of avoiding the costs and liability of their own plans, and they started encouraging their employees to switch over to 401(k)s. Eventually, standard pension plans became as scarce as hens' teeth...except for public employees."

"Right. And that includes all the politicians..., who take pretty good care of themselves, the last time I looked."

"You've got that right, Bob! Anyway, the net result of introducing 401(k)s was that it turned everyone into their own pension fund manager without bothering to tell them that inconvenient fact. So, now, they and they alone are responsible for making the right choices about what to invest in, what level of risk to accept, and what rate of return is required to achieve their goals. If they get it wrong, they're the ones who'll be paying the piper."

"That's precisely what's happened to Mom and Dad. And the only one who's gotten rich is the piper. They did what everyone else was doing, and just assumed that everything would take care of itself. But everything did *not* take care of itself, as we know, and that's why I'm talking to you now."

"Well, one thing Nicole and I learned at that seminar is that less than five percent of all professional money managers are able to match the S&P 500 returns in any one year..., and from one year to the next, it's never the *same* five percent.[*] If the pros do that badly, what chance do we amateurs have? It's insane to assume that ordinary folks like us can do a good job of managing our 401(k)s..., especially if we have a life."

"That life is gonna be a heck of a lot poorer, though, if they *don't* take the time to get involved in their own future."

"Bob, one of the most important principles we learned at that

---

[*]John Stossel, *Myths, Lies and Downright Stupidity: Get Out the Shovel—Why Everything You Know is Wrong* (New York: MJF Books/Fine Communications, 2009).

seminar is that the key to a successful retirement is *not* to build wealth, the way most people think, but to build cash flow. Think of a river instead of a pond. We also learned that houses are for living in, not for being piggy banks."

"Hold on there, Uncle Justin. Those two things sound good, but what exactly do they mean? Pond of money? Piggy banks?"

"Well, I could tell you, but Travis can explain it a lot better than I can."

"Who's Travis?"

"Travis Truepenny…. He's the one who led that seminar I'm telling you about. Now he's our Better Money Method advisor. He's shown us how to increase our retirement income by more than fifty percent. If you decide to meet with him, remember to ask about the pond of money and the piggy bank. He'll tell you a whole lot more, too. What I've said is just the tip of the iceberg."

"Listen, Uncle Justin, are you sure this method is really for someone *my* age? I'm hearing that it works great for you, but maybe I'm too young for this stuff."

"Well, I can see why you might think that. It's true that most of the people in Travis's seminar were in their fifties, sixties, and seventies…, and most of his clients are, too, from what I understand. But there was a twenty-five-year-old at that seminar, and Travis says that kid has gotten *amazing* results from the Better Money Method. In fact, according to Travis, this concept is so good that it'll work for anyone up to the age of *eighty*."

"But dad said it's too late for him and mom. And they're only in their mid-sixties."

"Your dad's a stubborn one, Bob…, always has been, since we were boys. I tried to get him into this thing ten years ago, and he wouldn't listen. Said it was harebrained. Now he sees it works, but he thinks he's too old. He's always been a genius at finding reasons *not* to do things. Listen, I'm not the expert on this. All I know is that it's worked beautifully for your Aunt Nicole and myself.... So go talk to the man who *does* have all the answers. It won't cost you a penny to hear him out. If you don't like what he has to say, you can always go down the path your dad took. How's that working out for him?"

"Not very well, unfortunately."

"Exactly.... I suggest you call Travis as soon as possible."

"Okay, but I have to admit, what you've been telling me so far does sound too good to be true."

"That's what *we* thought at the time, Bob. And we almost didn't do it. But then, one night, Nicole and I were watching the Discovery Channel, and they just so happened to have a show on about rats."

"Rats? What's that got to do with money?"

"Just listen a minute, and you'll see.... If you put a rat in a maze and give it some cheese out of a window when he pushes a lever, but then never give it cheese from that window again, he'll come back two or three times, and then give up. He'll never go to that window again. But if you do that with human beings, they'll come back over and over and over again. Just think of all those folks who play the one-armed bandits in Las Vegas. When I saw that TV program, I looked over at Nicole and said, 'We're smarter than rats, aren't we?' And she said, 'I sure would like to think so.' 'Well, then,' I said, 'why do we keep putting all this money in a 401(k) when it keeps going up and down like a yo-yo and makes us feel insecure about our retirement?'"

"I agree, Uncle Justin. I just don't know what to do instead."

"Well, your Aunt Nicole and I don't have any doubt about what you should do instead. You have to go with the Better Money Method. We checked it out, and it works. After a while, when our plan was in place for a time, I told my colleagues at the office about the method, and five of them agreed that it made sense, and they eventually set up their own plans. The others thought it was too good to be true and stayed with their 401(k)s."

"The old path of least resistance, eh?"

"Right. But you know what? A funny thing's happened during this market meltdown that has everyone else in trouble. Those of us who follow the Better Money Method haven't been the least bit concerned, because not one of us has lost a dime."

"Good for you, Uncle Justin!"

"Everybody else at work has been screaming bloody murder over their losses. And guess what? Recently, a few of them have been asking me how they could learn more about the Better Money Method. And just like with you, I've referred them to Travis. So, you better call him soon, young man, and set up an appointment, because he's a busy guy these days."

"Okay, I'll give him a call."

"Good thinking, Bob. And one more thing…. When you've learned all about this method, remember that it's not too late for your mom and dad to get onboard. If you reach the same conclusion Nicole and I did, maybe *they'll* finally see the light, too."

When Bob called Travis Truepenny to set up an appointment, it turned out that, just as Uncle Justin had said, Travis was a busy man indeed these days, so his schedule was booked for the next two weeks. That was okay with Bob, because it gave him plenty of time to think things through and sharpen up his questions. When the big day finally arrived, Bob was ready.

After the introductions, Bob said, "Before we go any further, Travis, I have a question for you that my Uncle Justin said you could answer far better than he could."

"What's that?"

"He said that when he attended your seminar, you told the group that a house is not a piggy bank. What does that mean?"

Travis smiled. "Bob, that's a great question, but it's gonna take me a little time to answer it properly, so bear with me. The reason I need some time to make my point is that you probably have a misconception that you share with ninety-nine percent of the population."

"I can hardly wait to hear what it is. As an attorney, I don't like to specialize in being wrong."

"Well, don't take this personally, Bob. There are powerful historical reasons, dating back to the Great Depression, why people think and behave certain ways when it comes to their money. Let me address your question by first asking *you* one. Why do you think it's so important to pay off your house?"

Bob looked puzzled. "That's an easy one. *Everybody* wants to pay off their house. Then they won't have to worry about losing it.... And when they retire, their expenses will be lower, since they'll no longer have to pay a mortgage. Isn't that self-evident?"

"Not to me.... To my way of thinking, those are emotional answers, not rational ones. As an attorney, you'll appreciate that distinction."

"I do, and I'm still waiting to hear your argument."

"You just said that by paying off your house you wouldn't lose it. You also said that by paying off your mortgage, your cost of living would be lower during your retirement."

"I did say both of those things, and I think they're indisputable."

"Well, counselor, we'll see if you still think so in ten minutes. I concede that both of those answers address deep fears that people have. No one wants to lose their house, for any reason. And no one wants to lower their standard of living when they get old. Now, do you know anyone in your own circle of friends and acquaintances who has lost their house through foreclosure?"

Bob thought about this for a moment. "No, I guess not..., although I've heard a lot about foreclosures on the news."

"But no one personally?"

"No."

"And do you know anyone who has a comfortable retirement because they paid off their house?"

"I certainly know people who have paid off their houses and are living comfortably in retirement, but I can't say that's *because* they paid off their houses."

"Right. If I asked people down on the street outside this building if they knew anyone who fit either of those profiles, ninety-nine percent of them would say no. Nevertheless, ninety-nine percent of them would probably agree with the two fears you mentioned and think it was prudent to act accordingly."

"I'm sure that's true. That's why I said they were self-evident…, at least, to most folks."

"Okay, let's take a closer look at why most people think they need to pay off their house as soon as possible.… Back in the 1920s, a nice house in this town cost about five thousand dollars. In fact, I can remember, when I was a kid, there was one house in our neighborhood that was nicer than all the rest, with a great view of the river and the city. One day, my grandpa told me that he had wanted to buy that house around 1923, but the owners wanted five thousand dollars for it, and there was no way he was going to pay that much for a house. Back then, the average annual income in this country was about fourteen hundred dollars, so to buy a house you either had to save up for several years or get a bank loan. It wasn't unlike today, except that mortgages back then had a clause in them that gave the bank the right to call in the loan at any time. This meant that the bank could contact the homeowner and demand that they pay off the loan in full at any time, and if you didn't, they could take your home from you, practically on the spot."

"That doesn't sound fair."

"Whoever said life was fair, Bob? Anyway, people knew that provision was in their loan, but they didn't worry about it because they had never heard of anyone being thrown out on the street, and they and the bank both knew that if the bank did anything like that, there was no way ordinary folks could pay off their loans. Now skip ahead six years from my grandpa eyeing that house to the stock market crash of October 29, 1929."

"Yeah, I've heard of that."

"I bet. So, just like other bubbles since then, there were a lot of average folks heavily invested in the market. After all, it had been going up for quite some time, so people figured it could never go down, and there was no way for them to lose. Unlike today, however, a large percentage of people were buying their stocks on margin. That meant it wasn't their money in the market, it was borrowed money…, money lent to them by their stockbrokers, who used something called a 'margin account.' For example, you could buy a hundred dollars' worth of stock by giving your broker just ten dollars in cash. Your broker would loan you the other ninety dollars through your margin account. So, when the market went down thirty percent, you had to come up with the difference. Your one hundred dollars of stock was now worth, say, seventy dollars, and you owed ninety dollars against it. That meant you could only borrow ninety percent of the new value, and ninety percent of seventy dollars is sixty-three dollars, so you owed the broker the difference between ninety dollars and sixty-three dollars…namely, twenty-seven dollars. When the broker made a 'margin call' to you for that twenty-seven dollars, you had twenty-four hours to come up with it. If you couldn't do that, the broker would start selling your stock, and would continue selling it until he got the account down to the agreed-upon balance. Most people didn't want to sell their stock when the market was down, figuring that that was the worst time to sell. So they went to their banks and withdrew enough cash to meet their margin call."

"I can see what's coming," said Bob.

"Yeah, with 20-20 hindsight, it's pretty easy now. But, back then, ignorance was bliss…, right up to the moment when it wasn't. As the market kept going down, people withdrew more and more cash from the banks over the next few months, which meant most banks started running out of cash. When word of that spread, there was a run on the banks. People started lining up, demanding their money, and to meet that demand, the banks started insisting that their borrowers pay off their mortgages in full. Since the homeowners didn't have that kind of cash on hand, the banks started foreclosing on the homes."

Stages of the Great Depression

"Why did they have to be paid off in full? Why couldn't they have asked, say, for the next three months' worth of payments?"

"For one thing, that wasn't an option in the contracts. For another, no one thought of it. When you're in a raft on the rapids, Bob, you don't have a whole lot of time to make decisions. In any case, that's how it played out. So, what do you think happened next? With very few buyers willing or able to pay cash for the homes, the banks quickly found themselves with virtually worthless real estate.

Then, lacking the cash to pay their depositors, many banks were forced to close their doors for good. And many investors in the stock market saw their holdings sold off by their brokers when they were unable to meet the margin calls. The net result of all that chaos was a massive downhill spiral. The brokers couldn't find anyone to buy the stocks, and the banks couldn't find anyone to buy the houses. That's what caused what we now call the Great Depression. Ultimately, the market fell more than seventy-five percent from its 1929 high to its 1932 low. In addition, more than half of the nation's banks failed, thousands of companies went bankrupt, and millions of Americans lost their jobs and their homes. What was once the American dream became the American nightmare. The only people who didn't lose their homes outright were the ones who had already paid them off."

"So, you see, Travis, I was right. It's good to pay off your home."

"It's true, they were able to keep a roof over their heads, but they still had to find a job and put food on the table. What good is it to own your house if you can't eat?"

"You have a point there."

"Most of us, as we were growing up, heard some version of this Great Depression story around the kitchen table, and that's where we all learned the mantra: 'Always pay off your home as quickly as possible, and own it outright.' But despite that, Bob, there are people in this country today who do *not* pay off their mortgage, even though they have the cash on hand to do so."

"Why would anyone place himself at risk like that?"

"They're not ignorant, that's for sure. To the contrary, based on my experience, they know *exactly* what they're doing. Even Warren Buffett has had mortgages in recent times, and he could have paid them off any day he wanted."

"Buffett could have even bought the *bank* that owned the mortgage!"

"Right. And what Buffett, and a lot of smart folks like him, have realized is that the rules have changed since the Great Depression. The hard lessons of the 1930s cannot be repeated, because certain safeguards have been put in place."

"Like what?"

"First of all, mortgages on homes no longer have a call provision in them. Your bank cannot call the mortgage due anytime it wants. The only time it can do that is if you stop making the payments. At that point, it's still required to give you the opportunity to catch up. Thus, successful investors know they're not running any abnormal risk by carrying a large mortgage. They also realize that mortgage interest is their best tax deduction, and they can earn a higher rate of return on their money than the cost of the mortgage. Furthermore, they know that a house appreciates in value over time, and that appreciation is the same, whether or not the house has a mortgage on it."

"I follow you so far. What other safeguards are there?"

"Well, stock margin accounts have been changed by law to require a minimum of fifty percent down. For some speculative stocks, such as in internet companies, brokers may even require their clients to put down eighty percent or more. This drastically reduces the risk that margin calls will get out of control."

"Any more safeguards?"

"Sure. In 1934, Congress created the Federal Deposit Insurance Corporation, or FDIC, to protect depositors' money in the banks. That eliminated the chance of a run on banks, because depositors know that the federal government is guaranteeing their money, up to some established limit per account. Furthermore, the Federal Reserve Bank has become more transparent and proactive than it was in the 1930s. During the Great Depression, the government added to the nation's economic problems by not providing the liquidity that the market and the banks needed. Compare that to how the government responded to the crash of 1987..., the first major stock market crash since 1929. Within *hours*, Alan Greenspan, the Chairman of the Fed, announced that it would supply as much cash as the nation's banks needed. This assured America and the world that there would be no repeat of 1929. In fact, most observers credit this action with preventing another 1929-style market crash…, and similar things happened in response to the market meltdown of 2008. The point of all this, Bob, is that people who say that you should pay off your house as soon as possible are using early twentieth-century 'wisdom' to make decisions in the twenty-first century, ignoring the vast changes that have occurred since then. In other words, the advice is based on fear, not knowledge."

"That's all fine and good, Travis, but I still can't see what's wrong with paying off my house as soon as possible."

"Alright, let me address that. What worries most folks is that if they lose their income for any reason, they'll also lose their house because they won't be able to keep up with the payments on the mortgage."

"Exactly."

"On top of that, they hate paying all that interest over the years. Their fear is legitimate, but their hatred is not. I'll give you a couple of examples to show why. I'm going to compare the traditional twentieth-century approach with what I call the twenty-first-century approach."

"Can you move beyond the theoretical and the hypothetical, Travis, and use some hard numbers?"

"I sure can. Let me write some numbers on the board here…. We've got Jack on this side, and Jill on the other. They both earn $50,000 a year, they both want to buy a town house close to work for $150,000, and they both have $50,000 in the bank. Jack wants to minimize his mortgage interest expenses and pay off his mortgage as soon as possible, so he makes a $45,000 down payment and gets a 15-year mortgage at 5.5%. His monthly payments are $857.94, but only 57% of that is tax-deductible interest; the rest is principal. Therefore, Jack's after-tax payment on his mortgage is $815.19 per month. Additionally, he sends in an extra $50 with each of his payments, all of which goes to the principal, providing no additional tax savings.

"Jill, on the other hand, gets a 30-year loan at 6% and makes only the required down payment of $30,000…, 20% of the purchase price. Her mortgage of $120,000 is bigger than Jack's of $105,000, but her pre-tax monthly payments of $719.46 are smaller than his of $857.94. However, that's not the whole story. Because 83% of Jill's monthly payment is interest, and therefore tax-deductible, her after-tax monthly payment is only $570.17, compared to Jack's $815.19…, a difference of $245.02 each month. She takes that $245.02, adds an extra $50 to it each month, and places the $295.02 into her savings. After five years, investing her money at 7%, Jill's $17,701.20 has grown to $18,543.99, plus she still has the $20,000 she didn't use for her down payment, which, at 7% interest, has grown to $28,352. That gives her a total of $46,894.99 for a rainy day account.

"Suddenly, Jack and Jill are both laid off from their jobs. Because Jack made a bigger down payment and has been sending in an additional $50 each month against his mortgage, he has more equity in his house than Jill has in hers—$73,832, compared to $30,604. But that won't help Jack to buy groceries or make mortgage payments. He's just learned a well-kept secret about home ownership: *A mortgage is a loan against your income, not a loan against your equity*. Since Jack is now unemployed, he is unable to access his home equity.

"Jill, on the other hand, has maintained ownership and control of her funds and now has $46,894.99 that she can access in an emergency. She doesn't need to panic over a job, because if she needs to, she can make her mortgage payments for more than five years without getting a job.

"Jack had better find a job, and do it quickly. But isn't it ironic, Bob? Jack's the one who made the large down payment, got a 15-year loan, and sent in an extra $50 every month, all to reduce his interest expenses and pay off his mortgage as fast as possible. Following his intuitive twentieth-century philosophy, he's the one at risk of losing his house and *all* of his equity..., while Jill does *not* come tumbling after. As we've seen, she's got five years before she has to worry about losing her house. She may have to flip burgers at McDonald's to put food on the table, but she's not going to get thrown out on the street, and she's not going to lose her equity.... I know that's a long answer to your question, Bob, but does it tell you why your Uncle Justin and I say that a house is not a piggy bank?"

"I'll give you that one, Travis. But I'm still skeptical and have a lot more questions. You've made me wonder, though, how many more of my 'self-evident' truths are going to bite the dust in this office."

"More than one, I'm afraid, Bob. At least, if I do my job right.... But let's take a ten-minute break, if you don't mind, so I can make a quick call to one of my clients."

"That's fine, Travis. I need to make a call of my own."

Chapter 3:

A Huge Scam

When Bob and Travis finished their phone calls, Bob said, "I know you're going to be making some specific recommendations for me today, Travis, but before you do, I'd like to ask you a few questions."

"Fire away."

"I have some thoughts about 401(k)s, but I'd like *your* take on them. In fact, that's the main reason I'm here."

"Well, Bob, I'll try to give you the short version on that, 'cause I could go on for hours. You may or may not know this, but many studies have shown that most folks don't really understand what they're getting into with 401(k)s. If they did, they wouldn't be going there, I can tell you that."

"Hold on, Travis. I know you don't mean to imply that a huge scam has been played on the American people. As Abraham Lincoln said, you can't fool all of the people all of the time."

"I thought it was P. T. Barnum who said that, but it doesn't matter. Whoever gets the credit also said that you can fool some of the people all of the time, and all of the people some of the time..., and my goal is to see that you're *never* among the fools."

"Thank you. That's *my* goal, too."

"Alright, let me begin to answer your question with a little historical context. In the period between the end of World War II and the 1960s, the U.S. economy was very robust, so most people had a secure job and most businesses prospered. However, the Great

Depression was still on the minds of a majority of Americans. The companies wanted to provide a secure retirement for their employees as a way to keep them loyal. The employees also liked this system because they had security, and they knew exactly what their retirement would look like when their working years ended. That system was known as a defined benefit plan. But then, in 1969, a serious business contraction hit the economy. There were bankruptcies, mergers, and receiverships of Wall Street firms, which caused a tremendous loss of consumer confidence. Congress was concerned about a possible 'domino effect.'"

"That sounds familiar," Bob said. "Does the world ever change?"

"I think the world changes, but people don't pay much attention to history. Anyway, Wall Street was becoming desperate, and other types of businesses were having serious challenges, so Congress thought it needed to act quickly. Wall Street responded to the economic contraction with discounted brokerage fees and no-load mutual funds. Wall Street was also looking for other solutions to regain its market share and to create some form of catalyst to get the American public investing again. So, what did it do? It sent lobbyists to Washington, and the lobbying resulted in the passage of a new set of retirement plan rules called ERISA, for the Employee Retirement Income Security Act."

"I once dated a girl with a name like that," Bob said. "The government sure likes those acronyms, doesn't it?"

"That's about the only thing they're good at.... And like all new laws, ERISA brought several changes with it. But the one that had the biggest impact was the introduction of the do-it-yourself retirement system known as the Individual Retirement Account. Most people just call it IRA. Under the original rules, an individual could put up to fifteen hundred dollars into an IRA account and get a tax deduction. That put Wall Street in a perfect position to 'help' Americans with this new retirement option. Wall Street got new investment dollars and started to regain the trust of the average American. After experiencing this new source of profit and realizing the fees to be earned on self-directed IRAs, Wall Street decided to get it all by controlling the lifetime retirement savings of every single American."

"There's no end to the greed on Wall Street, that's for sure."

"You can bank on it, Bob.... And, in the late 1970s, Wall Street got its wish with the birth of the 401(k). Now they could go straight into the workplace and set up shop, dealing directly with the HR departments to funnel the employees' savings right into Wall Street via payroll deductions."

"And no middle man."

"Middle men would only slow down the flow of cash into Wall Street. They don't want that. But the employers were pleased because they could eliminate the cost and the responsibility of the defined benefit plans..., which had served our grandfathers and grandmothers so well."

"I sure wish I had their options available to me."

"You're in good company there, Bob. You see, what happened was that the new plan gave Wall Street a virtual controlling hand over our money. In almost every case, employees are now unable to withdraw all their funds from their 401(k)s before they stop working, not because the law says so, but because the Wall Street contract says so. It's not the U.S. government that restricts your 401(k) money, it's Wall Street! That restriction gives Wall Street complete control of your money."

"I don't need big brother controlling my money. I can do that for myself, thank you."

"That's why you're here, I hope, Bob. Anyway, the defined benefit retirement has been replaced by what I call the Wall Street retirement plan..., more commonly known as the defined contribution plan. You get to send a defined amount of money to Wall Street, but there's no guarantee on your rate of return, and many costs are hidden. In fact, Wall Street is not required to disclose its managing fees."

"Wall Street certainly had Congress in its pocket on that one!"

"It's an unholy alliance from top to bottom between Wall Street and the government, Bob. But I have to admit, it started out pretty well. In fact, the period between 1980 and 2000 produced the longest bull market in U.S. history, and I think it's fair to call it the ERISA bull market. The new source of dollars produced impressive demands for stocks, and since their supply was limited, their price kept going up. However, the boom was not sustainable, and an artificial base devoid of sound fundamental investment principles fueled the market drop of 2001–2003. More and more financial writers today are starting to see the boom of the 1980s and 1990s as an aberration. There are no substantial data to support the notion that the market exuberance of those decades will return anytime soon. The ERISA bull market has run out of gas."

"I sure don't see any new baby boom generation on the horizon that will create another feeding frenzy like the last one."

"You got that right. But meanwhile a massive industry of so-called 'advisors' has grown up with a vested interest in the new status quo. Their plans are all structured to build assets under management for them to administer. The accounts are designed for the institutions that manage them and the government..., not you or your heirs. So, unless you happen to own stock in Fidelity or Bank of America or Edward Jones, or one of the other vendors, your interests are probably not going to coincide with theirs."

"But they sure do know how to create slick commercials to make you want to hand over your money, don't they, Travis?"

"Oh, they're master artists at that.... But what nobody tells you, including the employers, is, 'Hey, fella, you're on your own now. You're your own retirement planner.' The employers know that their employees could tell you all the statistics you'd ever want to hear about their baseball or football or basketball team, but they don't know squat about how their retirement plans work. So, they say to their employees, 'Oh, sure, we'll bring in a plan administrator from Merrill Lynch or someplace, once or twice a year, to explain things to you…. But whether you sink or swim is *your* problem.'"

"That sounds a lot like asking the average person to write his own will without knowing anything about the law. As an attorney, I can tell you that the odds of doing that right are between zip and zero."

"Absolutely right. The average person doesn't have the knowledge…, or the desire, for that matter…, to learn to be a pension fund manager. The result is that they have major misunderstandings and misconceptions about their 401(k) plans. Let me just go over the major ones with you."

"Okay, Travis. I suppose if you got to the minor ones, I'd have to move in here and pay you rent."

"That's true. I could go on about this forever. I hate scams. Now, first of all, 401(k)s lack liquidity. What do I mean by that? I mean that once you put your money in one of those things, it's damned hard to get it out again without a whole lot of strings attached."

"What kind of strings?"

"Well, there are government strings and company strings. Take your pick. One of the government strings is that you can't pull out any of your money without paying a penalty if you want or even *need* to do it before you get to the age of fifty-nine and a half."

"Aren't there some exceptions to that? Like for medical emergencies…, or going back to school…, or, in some plans, putting money down for your first house?"

"Yeah, there are some exceptions for that, and there's also something called a 72T, which allows you to take out money before you're fifty-nine and a half, provided you do it over a number of years and comply with the formula. I can see you know your law,

Bob. But most folks don't have medical emergencies, don't go back to school, and don't use their plans to buy a first house. On the other hand, plenty of folks get unemployed for a while or have a financial crisis and need to access their money before they turn fifty-nine and a half. And let me tell you, they pay *dearly* for that privilege."

"Okay…, and what's an example of a company string?"

"Oh, there are plenty of those. Companies can't be more lenient than the law, but they can certainly be more restrictive…, and many are. For example, I have a client who works for a major corporation, and when he saw all the disadvantages of his 401(k), he decided to stop putting any more money into it. He was even willing to pay the penalty for shutting it down altogether at the age of thirty-nine, but his employer wouldn't let him. In fact, his employer wouldn't let any of its employees shut down their 401(k)s at *any* age without quitting their jobs."

"That's sounds like a string to me alright."

"Exactly. And on top of the string section of this orchestra, most 401(k)s are dependent on the performance of the stock market. And we've all seen where *that's* gone recently."

"True, Travis, but I've always heard that as you get older, you should shift your profile from stocks to bonds…, fewer stocks and more bonds, to cut down the risk."

"The trouble with that theory, Bob, is that it's based on the premise that you can afford to lose your shirt when you're young because you have time to make the money back, whereas when you're old you don't. But if you don't have to, why should you lose money at *any* age? And with my system, which I'll describe to you in a few minutes, you won't ever lose money, no matter *how* badly the stock market performs."

"That sounds good to me!"

"The fact is, most people don't follow that advice about stocks and bonds anyway. They simply do what everyone else is doing, and then discover when it's too late that they don't have enough money for their retirement, so they stay in the stock market, hoping to make a higher return. It's kind of a fast-food approach to investing..., except you don't get fat."

"As in your bank account gets thinner and thinner?"

"You got it! Or maybe, in most companies, it's more like going to a Chinese restaurant. You know how they give you a choice of dinners..., one item from column *A*, and another from column *B*, and so on? Well, with the 401(k)s, a plan 'advisor' comes around to the company once or twice a year to tell you that you can have any combination of fund *A*, *B*, or *C*. *A* is most aggressive, *C* is least aggressive, and *B* is somewhere in-between. But because the 'advisor' gives the employees limited, if any, education at these supposedly 'educational' meetings, the employees usually just end up picking funds based on their gut feelings. It's like trying to pick a winning horse at the racetrack by how pretty it looks. And ninety-nine percent of the time, the funds the employees pick are invested in one or more mutual funds, because the plan 'advisor' tells them that this is the best place for their money in the long term. The theory is that professionals, who love to watch the stock market all day long, will be able to predict its ups and downs better than you can. But if that theory were true, Bob, why do ninety-five percent of the American public reach retirement age without enough money to maintain their lifestyle? Obviously, something's wrong with this picture. From my perspective, investing in the stock market is nothing more than gambling. It's a complicated amusement that is virtually impossible to beat in the long run."

"But if everyone felt that way, Travis, and no one ever invested a penny in the stock market, wouldn't the whole economy collapse?"

"Maybe, but everyone never *will* feel that way. Look at how many people buy lottery tickets, when their chances of winning are something like one in half a billion. The 401(k)s give better odds than that, but you and I can do far better still, Bob. Let everyone else take the risks, while we watch our retirement funds swell. As I said, the so-called 'advisors' tell folks that mutual funds are the best way to invest over the long run, and they have all these sexy names that would make anyone want to invest in them…, like the 'Follow the Green Line to Nirvana Fund.' They've convinced people that a successful fund is one that beats the market, not one that preserves your capital. How many times have you heard someone say, 'My fund did great. The market went down twenty-five percent, but I only lost twenty percent'?"

"In my young life, I've heard that several times already. Are you going to tell me there's an alternative to this?"

"You bet your boots, Bob! But before I get to that, I haven't finished telling you all the things that are wrong with the 401(k)s."

"You mean, there's *more*?"

"A *lot* more."

"Well, you've already persuaded me. But I'm ready to hear all the arguments you've got."

"Okay, another thing about 401(k)s that has always fascinated me is that business about your company matching your contributions. Have you ever heard people say, 'Take the matching, it's free money'? Or maybe they say, 'It's a guaranteed return on your funds even before you get started.' Ever hear that anywhere?"

"That's exactly what my HR guy told me two weeks ago."

"If that were true, Bob, there would be a lot more folks than there are who have a ton of bucks in their 401(k)s. Furthermore, there are no guarantees that the company will continue its matching policy *next* year. They can modify it, suspend it, or eliminate it anytime they want."

"So, they can entice me to participate in a 401(k) by offering me matching funds, then drop the offer down the road, and my money can be locked in as long as I continue to work for that company."

"That's about it, Bob. But there's more poison yet…, and this one's even more lethal, in my opinion. It's what they call administrative fees…, some of them open, but most hidden. When you look at them closely, they're a real eye-opener. When I ask people what fees they're paying for their 401(k) plan, a lot of them say, 'Nothing,' or, 'I don't know, but it can't be much.' The reality is, several studies have shown that the fees can easily exceed three percent.[*] Now, if you take three percent right off the top every year, it's going to have a dramatic long-term impact on reducing the amount you can build up in your 401(k). In fact, if you only take *two* percent off the top, it can literally cut your long-term return in half."

"I'd love to see the math on that."

"Well, get out your compound interest calculator, and be prepared to spend two hours on it, and I'll be glad to show you the numbers sometime. You know the old experiment with the frog and the hot water?"

"You mean the one about how if you throw a frog into hot water, he'll jump right out, but if you put him in cold water and then heat it up, he'll sit there till he boils?"

"That's the one. And these fund 'advisors' are doing the same thing to their clients. So long as they keep you sitting there, quietly boiling, they get to reap a percentage off your funds. Maybe that's why they like the phrase *long-term investment* so much."

"Okay, Travis, let's get to the bottom line. As I understand it, 401(k)s have two selling points. One is that your contributions are deducted from your current income, so you pay lower taxes now. The other is that, when you retire and start to take money out of the plan, your income will be lower, so you'll be in a lower tax bracket

---

[*]For example, see Matthew D. Hutcheson, "Uncovering and Understanding Hidden Fees in Qualified Retirement Plans," *Elder Law Journal*, 15, No. 2, 2007.

and consequently pay lower taxes. What's wrong with that argument?"

"It would be a great argument if it weren't for the inconvenient fact that it's totally false. The only way it could be true is if you were unsuccessful at saving."

"What exactly do you mean by that?"

"Well, obviously, if you're in poverty, your taxes will go down. But if you've been a successful saver, the chances are very good that your taxes will actually go *up* when you retire."

"You've gotta be kidding. Now you've gone too far, Travis. How could that be?"

"There are at least *four* reasons how that can be. First of all, you've probably paid off your house by the time you retire, so you can no longer get a deduction on your taxes for the interest you pay on the mortgage. Second, your kids are long grown…and hopefully out of the house…, so you can no longer get a deduction for *them*. Third, you're no longer contributing to your IRA or 401(k), so you don't get a deduction for *that*. And fourth, you're in fact taking money *out* of your IRA or 401(k), and that is being taxed as ordinary income. When you combine those four factors together, it can easily spell 'Higher Tax Bracket.'"

"What about the Roth IRAs, which allow you to pay your taxes now and take the money out tax-free later?"

"They're not bad as far as they go, but they don't go very far. They've solved part of the problem, but by no means all of it. And they come with strings attached, Bob. There are limits on who can have them, based on your income. There are limits on how much money you can put in them. There are limits on when you can take the money out of them without paying a penalty. And, like virtually all the other qualified plans, they're usually tied to the stock market, with all the weaknesses we've already discussed. I wouldn't even be surprised, when all is said and done, if they find a way someday to tax the Roths, too."

"To tell you the truth, Travis, it wouldn't be that hard for Congress to do that, because Roths, like all the other qualified plans, are just protected by laws, which Congress can change any time it likes…, unlike contracts, which are protected by the Constitution itself."

"I'll be getting to that very point a little later, Bob, but first I want to drive one final nail into the 401(k) coffin, and then we can move on…. Have you ever met anyone who thinks taxes will be *lower* in the future?"

"I can't say I have."

"It's ironic that most people project healthy returns for the growth of their retirement account, and at the same time they assume that their taxes will be lower when they retire. As we just discussed, that's based on their false assumption that they will necessarily be in a lower tax bracket. Furthermore, if you asked those same people if they think taxes in general will be going down in the future, you'd have very few takers, if any. You know how they say about a growing economy that a rising tide raises all boats?"

"Yeah, we've all heard that one."

"Well, the same thing can apply to taxes. They always go up, and never come down."

"They kinda defy Newton's Law, don't they?"

"Yeah, maybe in physics what goes up must come down, Bob, but certainly not in taxes. Given what's going on with out-of-control government spending and borrowing, I sure don't see any way taxes can do anything but go up in the future. So, the trick is to see to it that your retirement money goes to you and not to Uncle Sam."

"Actually, there are a lot of uncles on the state level, too…, and aunts, for that matter. I'm talking about the governors coming after us with their state taxes. Don't forget them."

"Don't worry, Mister Bedderoff, the state never lets me forget their taxes. And on top of that, there's the whole question of estate taxes. People with 401(k)s often end up with a lot of money in their accounts when they die, because they were afraid to take it out, for fear of being taxed or running out of cash. What they never realized is that once they die, that triggers an income tax on the whole amount that's left. Let's say you have half a million dollars in the account, and were taking out fifty thousand dollars a year to live on. That fifty thousand dollar income puts you in an effective tax bracket of, say, seventeen percent. But if you die next week, the entire half a million will be taxed all in one year, which will raise you to the highest tax bracket..., about thirty-six percent at the moment. So your heirs wind up getting a whole lot less."

"More of less, eh? Well, I'm only twenty-five, so I haven't been giving much thought to heirs just yet."

"True, but you're here to discuss your retirement plans, Bob, and ultimately those plans will affect a lot more people than you..., not least of whom will be the young lady you end up marrying one of these days."

"I do have someone in mind, you're right about that…. But tell me about your Better Money Method that Uncle Justin's so excited about. Is it anything like that software I see advertised on TV?"

"I very much doubt it. Which software?"

"The one that says I can track my own portfolio. They say it can predict trends in the market and notify me of the right time to buy and sell. That sounds good. Why can't I just do that myself?"

"Bob, anybody who tells you they can predict the market is either a fool or a liar. Even Warren Buffett says it can't be done."

"Several brokers say they'll send the software off to me for free. You can't beat that price."

"There are an awful lot of false prophets out there in the media, Bob. You've gotta be careful."

"I must admit, that part about free software did raise some red flags with me."

"I sure *hope* it raised red flags with you! You're a smart fellow, Bob…, what with your law degree and all. Do you think anyone's going to develop software and then just give it away to you for free? No strings attached?"

"I guess not."

"I guess not, too. Those raised flags should be rocketing out of your ears! When you were in law school, did they ever teach you anything about churning?"

"Sure. That's when financial advisors or money managers make trades in an account they have control over just to increase their sales commissions without profiting their clients. But the law came down real hard on that a few years back, so it's not the problem it used to be. Of course, it must go on here and there. Why do you ask?"

"Because, in my opinion, the software you're talking about is nothing more than a do-it-yourself stock-churning scheme. Since it's illegal for the stockbrokers to practice churning, they've gotten around the law by only 'providing' software that allows you to do the churning yourself. People even pay hundreds of dollars to go to seminars to learn all about it, and buy such software. But numerous studies have proven that the more often an individual investor trades his stock, the lower his rate of return. Nevertheless, these software programs, combined with drastically reduced trading costs, have turned thousands of people into glorified day traders."

"With computers and the internet, Travis, they can even do it at night."

"True. But I think, at best, it's really nothing more than a game for bored retired people…, and at worst it's another example of folks trying to grab the brass ring without doing any real work. If that software could really do what they say, why wouldn't the developers just program it to buy and sell at the right time?"

"I thought that's what they *were* doing."

"No. There's a key difference here that you're missing. Their program tells *you* when to buy or sell. It doesn't do the buying and selling itself. And, of course, they have all the usual disclaimers to cover their own butts if you lose money by following their program's advice. Think about it, Bob. If those developers could create a program that knew when to buy and sell in the market with one hundred percent accuracy…, or even fifty-point-one percent accuracy…, they wouldn't need *you* at all. They could just go sit on the beach someplace, drinking margaritas, and let the profits roll in. That would be a whole lot easier than running all those ads and teaching those seminars. In fact, do you know a *single person* who's making a killing by using that kind of software?"

"No, I don't."

"I would've been shocked if you had said anything else."

"Well, Travis, there's always the option of going to one of those big wire houses like Merrill Lynch, Charles Schwab, or Edward

Jones. They all have good financial advisors, don't they?"

"You sure would think so from their ads. Every day, on TV, in magazines, on the internet, and in their own brochures, they proudly proclaim their expertise. And they've got great-sounding tag lines…, like *'Independent advisors with the freedom to serve their clients….'* Or, *'We beat our Lipper Average….'* Or *'The knowledge and experience of a global investment firm.'* Or my current favorite, *'Just stay on the green line….'* I could go on and on."

"You're right. There's no end to them."

"But that's all they are…, great tag lines. I know they sound enticing, but that's the work of Madison Avenue, not Wall Street. What you really need to understand is the fine print. For example, do you know what 'We beat our Lipper Average' means?"

"No."

"It means, they beat the average for their fund classification. Is that what you want? Someone who just beats the average for their fund classification? You want to be a C student, Bob?"

"No, from what I've seen, beating their fund average is not much of an accomplishment."

"That's the understatement of the year. And, to add insult to injury, the average mutual fund only earns about fifty-seven percent of what the S&P 500 does. But let's get back to that fine print I mentioned. Have you ever taken a close look at one of those broker agreements?"

"I've read a lot of fine print, but never in broker agreements."

"Okay, read it here."

"It's pretty tiny, Travis, but I can just make it out. It says, 'Your account is a brokerage account and not an advisor account. Our interest may not always be the same as yours.' That sounds like they're going to take care of themselves, and to hell with me."

"That's how I read it, too. And what does the next sentence say?"

"It says, 'Please ask us questions to make sure you understand your rights and our obligations to you, including the extent of our obligations to disclose conflicts of interest and to act in your best interest.'"

"What do you make of that, Bob?"

"That's the kind of clause that covers their backside if we end up in court."

"Precisely. And it clearly indicates that there's an inherent conflict of interest between them and you. Do you have clauses like that in your contracts with *your* clients, Bob?"

"Absolutely not. Attorneys are not supposed to have adversarial relationships with their own clients."

"Alright. We're almost there. Just read the next two sentences in that fine print."

"Okay. It says, 'We are paid both by you and, sometimes, by people who compensate us based on what you buy. Therefore, our profits, and our salespersons' compensation, may vary by product and over time.'" Wow!

"Wow is right! So, what does *that* tell you, counselor?"

"It's no wonder the brokers make so much money, and the clients make so little. They're telling us right here that their so-called advisors are dishing out nothing more than sales pitches for products of the day so they can get a fat commission from someone."

"Now you can see why they make the print so small..., and then bury it at the back somewhere."

"If I signed this contract, Travis, I would basically be signing away my right to go after them if and when they screw me. If I ever tried to take them to court, they would use that very paragraph I just read as Exhibit A against me.... So, despite all their fancy brochures and TV ads saying what great advisors they are, they're really nothing more than supermarkets for financial products."

"I guess I've gotten my message across, Bob. The fact is, there are a lot of sales jobs that require deep knowledge of the product, but being a broker is not one of them. Let me tell you a story about that."

"Another one of your depressing anecdotes?"

"I just tell the facts, my friend."

"I know you do..., even when they hurt."

"Sorry, Bob, I've got mirrors in my house. I wouldn't be able to look into them if I didn't tell people the truth as I see it.... Anyway, a friend of mine who's a mortgage broker told me recently about a woman he hired a couple of years ago to write mortgages. He said she had a great personality and people loved her, but he finally came to the conclusion that she was never really going to get a good handle on financing and how money works, so he let her go. Then he looks at me and says, 'Guess what she's doing now? She's a financial advisor for Edward Jones!'"

"I guess that says it all, Travis."

"Well, not quite. I do have a couple of other points I want to cover. First of all, have you ever noticed what the big wire houses do when there's a market meltdown? Merrill Lynch, Fidelity, Vanguard, and all the others?"

"Is there *one* thing they all do?"

"Well, stop and think about it for a minute.... Do they change their products to make them more competitive? Do they reduce their fees? Do they eliminate some of the risks in their products? No, they just up their marketing campaign and give their products sexier names."

"Another case of Madison Avenue rescuing Wall Street, eh?"

"Exactly. It drives me crazy that rather than clean up their act, they just come out with a new, glitzier marketing campaign to suck you back into the rabbit hole. I guess it's because they make money on the up *and* the down side. They get paid while you're happy with the market and buying more stocks, and they get paid again when you're *un*happy with the market and selling your stocks."

"I can't think of too many other professions, Travis, where you win even when you lose."

"That's because the brokers are *not* losing. Only their clients are."

"True."

"There's a saying, Bob: 'The broker made money..., the advisor made money..., two out of three ain't bad.'"

"Very funny. Unless *I'm* the third one.... And that brings me to my next question, Travis."

"You like asking questions as much as I like telling stories!"

"I guess you're right. Anyway, I wanted to ask you about annuities. Aren't they supposed to take the risk out of investment? What do you know about them?"

"Good question. There are several reasons why annuities are popular. One is that they can provide a monthly stream of income during retirement that will never dry up. A lot of people are already used to receiving their income on a monthly basis, so they like that arrangement. Also, annuities come from insurance companies, and people like that because insurance companies have a long track record of being safe."

"Wait a minute there.... What about AIG? They're the biggest insurance company in the world, and the government had to bail them out, not too long ago."

"Well, it wasn't the insurance wing of AIG that was sick. It was the mortgage department, with all its derivatives and other speculative games they were playing to satisfy their greed. The insurance wing was and *is* doing just fine. That's because insurance companies are required to have a hundred and five cents for every dollar of liability, while banks are only required to have five cents."

"Oh, I didn't know that."

"Most people don't.... But to get back to annuities, there are three kinds, and two of them are good. In this case, two out of three ain't bad is true. *Fixed* annuities are tied to very conservative portfolios, such as triple-A bonds, and you get paid a low but dependable rate of return...., something like four or five percent."

"That's still better than your typical CD at the bank, Travis."

"Right, that's what people like about them. But there's another good kind of annuities known as *indexed*..., which means that you get paid a rate of return that's pegged to an index such as the S&P 500. That allows you to profit from the growth of the market without actually being invested *in* the market."

"That's interesting. So, that takes out all the risk?"

"Well, they have a cap on the upside and a floor on the downside. For example, most indexed annuities will place a cap of, say, seven percent on the market gain. So, if the market goes up twelve percent, you still only earn seven percent. On the other hand, if the market goes down twenty percent, most annuities have a floor of zero percent, and some have a floor of one or two percent.... So, in a worst-case scenario, you'll earn nothing in a given year, but that's better than going down twenty percent."

"That sounds good to me, Travis. I'd gladly give up making a killing on the upside if I can be guaranteed an above-average rate of return in the worst of times."

"Yes, a zero rate of return is definitely better than a minus rate of return. By limiting the risk on the downside, an indexed annuity, even though it has a cap on it, will give you a better than average rate of return in the long run."

"Okay, Travis. Now, before you tell me about the bad kind of annuity, I'd like to know which of these two good kinds you prefer."

"Well, if my only options were to buy some kind of annuity, I would go with the indexed kind because, in the long run, I will do better than the four or five percent that the fixed kind will give me. Nevertheless, I recognize that some people may prefer the steady returns that you get with the fixed annuities."

"Alright. I guess I'm ready to hear about the bad kind."

"The bad kind is called *variable* annuities. You can lose your shirt with these because your money is actually invested in mutual funds in the stock market…, with all the risks that we've discussed earlier."

"After talking to you, I'm *definitely* not going there."

"Right. And on top of that, investing in mutual funds increases the administrative costs of variable annuities by approximately three percent…, so these annuities have to make three percent more than any other ones just to break even."

"If they're as bad as you say, why would anyone ever want one?"

"We're back to the gambling issue. Some folks just love to gamble with their money. The lure of making big bucks draws them in, and they ignore the fact that they can also *lose* big bucks. For my part, I wouldn't touch them with a ten-foot pole."

"Okay, variable annuities are out. Is there anything else I should know about the fixed and the indexed ones?"

"Well, the interest earned in annuities grows taxed-deferred. That's true of *all* three kinds. People like that, but as we saw earlier, the attraction is based on the idea that you'll be in a lower tax bracket after you retire, which may not be the case."

"Are there any other downsides to owning an annuity that I'm not aware of? Knowing you, there *must* be."

"Yeah, there are at least two more. One that I consider a serious downside is that, just like IRAs and 401(k)s, they lack liquidity. Most of them have a penalty if you want to get money out of them early..., and if you take out more than you put in, your interest earned is taxed. If you *do* keep it all in until you retire, and then use it for your retirement income, it's taxed LIFO."

"Lie-foe? What's that?"

"Last in, first out. It means that if you take some money out of your annuity, the government considers that money to be the interest you've earned on the account, and taxes it as ordinary income. And it does that right up to the point where you're no longer taking money out of the interest you've earned, but from the principal itself."

"Can you put some numbers on that?"

"Sure. Let's say, you have $500,000 in your annuity, and $400,000 of that is principal, with the remaining $100,000 being the interest you've earned over the years. If you should want to take $120,000 out of the account, the government will tax the $100,000 that you earned in interest, and let you have all of the remaining $20,000 tax-free."

"So, even the best kinds of annuities seem to have more drawbacks than I anticipated. You've also talked me out of going down the 401(k) road and the do-it-yourself investment advisor road. And I wouldn't go near those TV-advertised get-rich-quick software schemes. Where does that leave me? Are you ready to tell me about the Better Money Method yet?"

"Why don't you give your mind a little rest, Bob. Then you'll be fresh when we start the good news. It's not that complicated, but it will take a while to explain. When's the next time you have some time to spend here?"

"How about tomorrow?"

"Sorry, Bob. Tomorrow's too soon for my calendar. How about a week from tomorrow?"

"A week from tomorrow it is."

Chapter 4:

Too Good to Be True

When Bob arrived at Travis's office, the following week, he had a young woman with him.

"Travis," he said, "this is Becky, my girlfriend. I've been telling her some of your ideas, and she wanted to hear them for herself."

"Frankly," Becky said, "I've been doing just about everything you've been telling Bob is wrong. All I've been hearing from him secondhand is gloom and doom…, although I must admit I haven't yet been able to find any holes in your arguments. I thought I'd better come in and hear the story from the horse's mouth."

"I've been compared to other parts of a horse, Becky, but never to its mouth."

"Sorry, Travis, I didn't mean that literally."

"That's alright. I'll accept the mouth."

"He likes to talk, Becky," Bob said. "Fortunately, what he says makes a lot of sense. I went out of here last week a bit depressed, I must admit, Travis. So, now I'm eager to hear you talk about your Better Money Method to brighten up my mood."

"Mine, too," said Becky.

"Okay, guys, if I told you the Better Money Method could get you rates of return on your investments that meet or exceed those achieved by the top five percent of investment money managers in this country, what would you say?"

Becky brightened. "I'd say, 'Go for it!'"

"And what would you say if the Method would let you eliminate all risk of market loss and increase your retirement income by at least fifty percent over any of the 'traditional' plans?"

Bob smiled. "I'd say I'd sleep like a baby at night during market meltdowns. And during the days, I'd come over here and kiss the ground you walk on."

"Well, you can save the kisses for Becky, Bob.... As for the Better Money Method, it's based on what I call the four pillars.... One, avoid market losses.... Two, invest based on sound knowledge.... Three, have a specific plan for the next market crash.... Four, have a sound exit strategy."

"Well, Travis, those are pretty words," Bob said, "but how do I know you're not just another TV snake oil salesman?"

"Your Uncle Justin sent you to me, didn't he?"

"He sure did."

"And he's doing great, following my advice, isn't he?"

"That's what he says."

"So, that should answer the snake oil question."

"Actually, I believe that *you* believe what you're telling me,

Travis. The trouble is, I don't see how it's possible to achieve all of your four pillars. Frankly, I don't even see how you can achieve *half* of them. If you can do that, you've got a client here for life!"

"My favorite kind! Okay, future client for life…, and maybe *two*…, let's get started with the four pillars. The first one is avoiding market losses. Have either of you ever heard Warren Buffet's rules of investing?"

Becky shook her head.

Bob thought for a moment. "I may have," he said, "but I don't recall. What are they?"

"There are only two of them. The first one is, *Never lose money*. And the second one is, *Never forget rule number one*."

"Very funny," Becky said. "So, we get two rules for the price of one."

"Actually, you get one rule for the price of two."

"You're quite a wit, Travis."

"Thank you, Becky…. Now, the best tool I have to accomplish Buffet's rules is known as an indexed universal life insurance policy."

Becky frowned. "That's a mouthful."

"Well, we call them IULs, for short."

"Travis," Bob said, "I know what a life insurance policy is. And you'll explain the indexed part, I'm sure. But why is it called universal?"

"Because the policies are so flexible. And you're right, I'll get to the indexed part in a bit. For the moment, let's stay with the first pillar, avoiding market loss. IULs have some powerful ways to help us do just that. Basically, they use a couple of little known concepts, which nevertheless have been tested over time."

"Uncle Justin never mentioned IULs."

"He had to leave *something* for me to tell you about, Bob. Justin likes a man to earn his keep, so let me earn mine…. Universal Life policies, the predecessors of *Indexed* Universal Life policies, have been around since the Seventies.... But back then they were mainly used by the rich to protect their money. Someone who legally should have been in the eighty or ninety percent tax bracket at that time could shelter his money so cleverly that he didn't pay any taxes at all."

"That's Un-American," Becky said with a big smile.

"It's what I call being poor on paper. The Better Money Method lets *everyone* be poor on paper..., including both of *you*. But I'll come back to that later."

"We won't let you forget that one," Bob said.

"Actually, I'm not surprised, Bob, that your Uncle Justin didn't mention IULs to you, because he knows that most people wouldn't have the slightest idea what he was talking about. I've done market studies that show the average American has never heard of IULs."

"You've actually researched that?" Becky asked.

"I sure have."

"You don't miss a trick, do you, Travis?"

"I try not to, Becky. Anyway, those market surveys show that once people are introduced to IULs, their first reaction is, 'They're too good to be true.' And their second reaction is, 'If they're true, I want one!'"

"Convince me," said Bob.

"Me, too," Becky agreed. "I'm all ears."

"Alright, let's get back to those little known concepts I was going to tell you about. The first one is that an IUL allows you to get the benefit of participating in the up side of the market without taking any of the downside risk."

"Isn't that the same thing you were talking about last week, when you explained indexed annuities?" Bob asked. "As I recall, you said they have a cap and a floor, so they give investors some of the upside gain in years when the market goes up, but the floor protects them from loss when the market goes down."

"That's true. But while more and more folks are learning about indexed annuities, most of them have no idea you can do the same thing with an IUL..., only *better*."

"How *much* better?" Becky asked.

"A *lot* better. Most IULs have a higher cap than annuities do."

"When you say most," Bob said, looking skeptical, "do you mean some of them *don't?*"

"That's exactly what I mean. Sure, like everything else in the world, there are some bad IULs out there. But it's my job to steer you to the best ones."

"Not even the *good* ones..., the *best* ones," Becky said. "I like that."

"You're supposed to. So, here's how it works. In the years when the market goes up, you'll receive a higher rate of return than you would with an annuity, for at least two reasons. The caps will be higher..., between fourteen and sixteen percent, compared to, say, seven percent..., and the costs and the taxes will be lower."

"That's all well and good, Travis," Bob said, "but this capping business doesn't seem to be ideal for those years when the market does really well. The caps would keep me from making a killing."

"In this state, Bob, you can get the death penalty for murder.... But more seriously, I mostly hear that objection from financial planners. What they don't realize is that when you put a cap of fourteen percent on your gains, and a floor of zero under your losses, you're going to do better, in any thirty-year period, than you would if you had no cap and no floor."

"Can you put some numbers on that, Travis?" Becky asked. "It always makes more sense to me when I can see the figures."

"Sure. Let's say you put $100,000 into an S&P 500 fund in a 401(k) in 1980.... At the end of 2009, thirty years later, after fees have been deducted, you would have approximately $980,000. But if you had put the same $100,000 into one of the IULs I recom-mend..., at the end of 2009, after fees have been deducted, you would have approximately $1.3 million."

"I could think of a lot of things to do with that extra three hundred and twenty thousand dollars," Becky said.

"It's better than that, Becky."

"How so?"

"Because, in the first scenario, when you take cash out of your 401(k), all of that is taxable as ordinary income. So, when Uncle Sam is finished taking his share, you'll be lucky to end up with $750,000 of your money."

"That sounds about right," Bob said.

"An IUL, on the other hand, is funded like a Roth IRA. Your original $100,000 was after-tax money, and everything you've earned in the policy is tax-free. Therefore, at the end of the thirty years, you get to keep the *whole* $1.3 million."

"That's close to *twice* as much," Becky said. "$1.3 million, com-pared to $750,000."

"And that's assuming that taxes don't go *up* in the future," Travis added.

"I wouldn't bet on that," Bob said.

"My job, guys, is to see to it that you don't bet on *anything*.... Now let me introduce you to the second great feature of IULs..., a little sweetheart known as lock and reset."

"You sure use a lot of unfamiliar terms, Travis," Becky said. "What in the world is lock and reset?"

"The name refers to what happens to your money at the end of each year. If you've had a positive market gain, it gets locked in as principal at the end of the year. And that principal is contractually guaranteed against any future loss. In other words, the principal can *never* be reduced because of market loss.... That's the lock part."

"And what's the reset part?" Becky asked.

"Well, with the start of the new year, you get a new zero point. So, if the market went down the previous year, you don't have to climb back up to zero before you gain. Instead, you start at zero, and any gain goes into your plus column, up to your cap."

"What if the market went *up* the previous year?" Bob asked.

"Same thing. All your gain from the previous year, up to your cap, gets locked in as principal, and that's your new zero point."

"When you say, 'at the end of the year,'" Bob asked, "do you mean December 31?"

"No, the year starts when your money is credited into the insurance company, and ends three hundred and sixty-five days later."

"What about leap years?" Becky asked with a wicked grin.

"You're a sly one, Becky. In a leap year, if you started on February twenty-ninth, you would only get one-fourth of the return that everybody else gets."

"You're kidding."

"Of course, I am. In a leap year, the end would come on the following February twenty-eighth."

"If you two jokers are finished with your nonsense," Bob said, "I have a serious question.... Do indexed annuities have the same lock and reset provision?"

"Yes, they do. But, as I mentioned earlier, the IULs I prefer have higher caps."

"That's right. You said they have caps of fourteen to sixteen percent, compared to around seven percent for the indexed annuities. That's quite a difference, Travis. How in the world can insurance companies afford that?"

"The simple answer, Bob, is that they invest your money. But that takes some explanation. Have you ever heard of whole-life policies?"

"I've heard of them, but I don't really know anything about them."

"Bob's only twenty-five, Travis," Becky said, "so he hasn't given a lot of thought to life insurance up till now. Neither have I."

"Well, you will from here on out, I promise you that.... Anyway, whole-life insurance policies are what come to most people's minds when they think about permanent life insurance..., as opposed to term insurance, which only covers a specific period of time, usually five or ten years. Whole-life insurance came out decades before IULs, so people tend to know a lot more about them. When you buy a whole-life policy, it has a dividend between four and five percent per year."

"That sounds like a good return to me," Becky said. "Especially these days."

"It does sound good, doesn't it? But it isn't, and I'll tell you why.... The cost of whole-life insurance is higher than for the IULs I advocate, and the four to five percent so-called 'dividend' is not a dividend at all. Even the IRS has figured that one out. It doesn't tax those so-called 'dividends' because it realizes that they're actually refunds for overpayments for the insurance. What the companies do is charge you more than they should, and then 'give' you a 'dividend.'"

"That sounds like something Bernie Madoff would have come up with!" Bob said.

"Yeah, it kinda does. To be honest, though, it's been around a lot longer than Madoff and his scams. But let me answer your question about how the insurance companies can put the caps so high on IULs. First of all, you need to understand that buying life insurance is a lot like buying a car. You can get a Mustang stripped down with a six-cylinder engine and minimal trim, or you can get one with a suped-up V-eight, a beefed-up suspension, and fancy trim. At either end of the extreme, it's still a Mustang. Same chassis underneath. Life insurance is a lot like that."

"How so?" Becky asked.

"If you really understand it, *all* life insurance is term insurance with or without something thrown over the top."

"Wait a minute, now," Bob said. "How can whole-life insurance be a form of term insurance? By definition, whole-life insurance has no end date, and term insurance does."

"Sure, but with whole-life insurance, the companies calculate how long a person is likely to live, and then they, in effect, create a term policy around that. But with both term and whole-life insurance, the companies figure out level payments…, which are, in fact, averages of what the person would have to pay in the early, middle, and late years. Without level payments, the premiums would go up every year, and people don't like that. Insurance companies take your overpayments in the early years, invest that money, and make a profit. They've figured out that they need about two percent in profit and overhead to stay in business. If they make more than that…, say, six percent…, they'll credit the four percent difference to your account to offset increased payments in the future."

"That all sounds good, Travis," Becky said. "Are there any downsides to whole-life policies?"

"You're too young to remember this, Becky, but back in the Sixties, consumer advocates, like Ralph Nader, persuaded people that whole-life insurance was a bad investment, for two reasons. First, the cost of the insurance itself is very high. Second, as I said before, the 'dividends' are really just refunds of overpayments. So, instead of buying whole-life insurance, said the consumer advocates, people should buy term insurance and invest the difference."

"I've heard that phrase," Bob said.

"That's right. It's still the mantra of all the talking heads. But the problem, Bob, is this: what do most people *do* with the difference?"

"I assume they don't invest it. Maybe they buy the latest phone, or big-screen TV, or something like that."

"Maybe. In any event, the concept of buying term insurance and investing the difference sure hasn't done anything to help people better understand financial management.... So, back in the Seventies, after that concept became so popular, a company by the name of E. F. Hutton got to looking at the fact that most insurance companies were paying a decent rate of return on their annuities, but a much lower rate of return on their whole-life policies. Then E. F. Hutton discovered that the tax laws allowed some special benefits to life insurance that annuities didn't have. So, they approached some of the insurance companies with the idea that the companies should provide a higher rate of return on life insurance…, at least equal to what they were paying on the annuities, if not better. That way, they said, life insurance policies would be a good place for people to park their money for future growth."

"And what did the companies say?" Becky asked.

"I wasn't there, Becky, but I can just imagine the conversation. Someone from Hutton says, 'Why don't you guys offer a higher rate of return on your life insurance contracts, so the public can take advantage of these special tax features?' And the insurance company guy replies, 'Well, that's an interesting concept. I'll get back to you on that.' And then they never said another word about it."

"Why not?"

"Because, back then, Becky, the concept of buy term and invest the difference was just taking off, and term insurance was probably the most profitable product the companies offered…. In fact, it still *is*, to this day…, because they only pay out a death benefit on about one percent of all the people who buy the policies."

"So, they figured," said Bob, "why fix something that isn't broken? They were swimming in money, so why change anything?"

"Exactly. But then the people at E. F. Hutton did something very interesting. They didn't take the rebuff sitting down. Instead, they bought their own life insurance company and introduced the very first universal life insurance policy. But back then the game was played a little differently than it is now. In the Seventies, a client could buy, say, $5,000 worth of life insurance, and then put $1 million into the policy. For round numbers, let's say you earned 10% annual interest on that, which would come to $100,000. The insurance company would then deduct the cost of the $5,000 death benefit, which would be about $200 a year, so your tax-free income would be $99,800. Needless to say, people with wealth…, who back then were in the 80% to 90% tax bracket…, really liked that concept, and that form of tax shelter took off like a rocket. Then along came the IRS, who was obviously unhappy with this arrangement, and they took the matter to the Supreme Court, hoping to have it declared illegal. But the Court ruled against the IRS."

"I read that decision in law school," Bob said. "It had to do with the irreversibility of contracts. Under the *ex post facto* provision of the Constitution, neither Congress nor the courts can undo a contract that was legal at the time it was signed. They can change the rules for future contracts, but not for past ones."

"Right," said Travis. "So, in the Eighties, Congress came up with three sets of laws, known as TEFRA, DEFRA, and TAMRA,* to try to address what they perceived as tax loopholes. The bottom line of all those laws came down to two things. First, they said if you were going to buy life insurance, it had to at least *look* like life insurance."

"What does that mean?" Becky asked.

"It means that Congress specified minimum death benefits, based on the amount of money you want to put into the policy. So, you could no longer buy a $5,000 policy and put $1 million into it."

"How much can you put in now?"

"It all depends on your age, gender, and health. Also, there has to be a realistic connection between the amount of the death benefit and the economic damages your heirs would actually suffer if you were suddenly to die. There are complex formulas for all of this. Done correctly, it's very much tailored to each individual."

"Okay," Bob said, "I think we understand all that. Don't we, Becky?"

---

*TEFRA: Tax and Fiscal Responsibility Act (1982); DEFRA: Deficit Reduction Act (1984); TAMRA: Technical and Miscellaneous Revenue Act (1988).

"I think so. What was the second point of the new laws, Travis?"

"The second point was that you can't put all the money into the policy in one year. Depending on your age, you must invest it in no less than four to five years."

"What's the reason for that?" Bob asked.

"So you can't shelter your money all at once. That way, Uncle Sam has a chance to grab some of it."

"Well, then, Travis," Becky said, "if Congress has knocked the stuffing out of your precious IULs, why do you still think they're so attractive?"

"Because they left some stuffing in there. The thing is, these plans are complicated, and you need someone competent to make sure you comply with all the tax laws to get all the goodies you're after. The problem is, most people are lazy…, and that includes most financial planners and insurance agents. They don't want to take the time to learn something new, when they can just keep doing what they already know. In effect, they say, 'These new rules are too complicated. I'm just gonna keep selling term insurance, because it's really easy to sell. Everyone understands that insurance is a bad investment, so buy term and invest the difference.' That's why IULs have been around for at least fifteen years, and the average American has never heard of them."

"Well," Bob said, "for the last two or three years, our economy's grown very slowly, well below our historic averages. Now that the nation has voted to keep the same leaders, I'm afraid we'll have an extended period of anemic growth, much like Europe's. How will your IULs perform in that kind of market?"

Travis grinned. "The lock and reset," he said, "is magic in that situation. When the economy gets anemic, as you say, people's first impulse is to pull back. But even in markets like that, there are periods of ups and downs. The beauty of the lock and reset is that it allows you to capture some or all of the ups and avoid all of the downs."

"Can you give us some concrete examples, Travis?" Becky asked.

"Sure. Let's look at Japan's Nikkei 225. For the twenty years between 1989 and 2009, that index was mostly a bear market. Its all-time high occurred on December 29, 1989, at the peak of the Japanese economic bubble, closing on that day at 38,915.87. That represented a sixfold increase during the previous decade. But by twenty years later, on March 10, 2009, it had dropped almost 82 percent to 7,054.98. To put that in perspective, if you invested a thousand dollars in the Nikkei in 1989, by 2009 that would have shrunk down to 222.02."

"Really?!" Bob said. "*That* bad?"

"That bad. Take a look at this table."

The Value of $1,000 in the Nikkei 225
vs. an IUL with a Floor of Zero and a Cap of 15%

Year	Year-End Close	Annual Return	Value of $1,000 in Nikkei	IUL Value
1989	32,839.00	NA	$1,000.00	$1,000.00
1990	29,980.00	−8.71	$912.94	$1,000.00
1991	26,292.00	−12.30	$800.63	$1,000.00
1992	19,346.00	−26.42	$589.12	$1,000.00
1993	18,591.00	−3.90	$566.13	$1,000.00
1994	19,112.00	2.80	$581.99	$1,028.02
1995	16,140.00	−15.55	$491.49	$1,028.02
1996	21,407.00	32.63	$651.88	$1,182.22
1997	18,003.00	−15.90	$548.22	$1,182.22
1998	16,527.00	−8.20	$503.27	$1,182.22
1999	15,836.59	−4.18	$482.25	$1,182.22
2000	20,337.00	28.42	$619.30	$1,359.55
2001	12,999.70	−36.08	$395.86	$1,359.55
2002	11,024.94	−15.19	$335.73	$1,359.55
2003	7,972.71	−27.68	$242.78	$1,359.55
2004	11,715.39	46.94	$356.75	$1,563.49
2005	11,668.95	−0.40	$355.34	$1,563.49
2006	17,059.66	46.20	$519.49	$1,798.01
2007	17,287.65	1.34	$526.44	$1,822.03
2008	12,525.54	−27.55	$381.42	$1,822.03
2009	7,290.96	−41.79	$222.02	$1,822.03

"Well," Becky said, "it's clear to me that neither of you guys has ever heard of taking a break. Bob, let's go look over that Italian restaurant down the street…, and if we like it, we can take Travis out to lunch later."

"Oh, you'll like it, alright," Travis said. "They've got great food there…. See you back here in, say, half an hour?"

"Half an hour it is," Bob said.

Chapter 5:
The Dumbest People I Know

"We got you a cappuccino, Travis," Becky said, "with a big foamy head on it."

"Mighty nice of you."

"Becky and I were talking," Bob said. "It's clear to us, from everything you've said, that you're highly knowledgeable and not a bit lazy, unlike some of those other agents you described. But before I sign on the dotted line with you, we had a question. And then I want to go over a few points you made earlier."

"Alright."

"Do any insurance companies sell both annuities *and* IULs?"

"To the best of my knowledge, all the companies that sell IULs, including all the best ones, also sell annuities."

"Well, then, why would they sell an inferior product when they have a superior one?"

"For the same reason that Ford sells Lincolns and Fords, Bob. Or why the ice cream parlor down the street sells sundaes, and not only scoops of plain vanilla.... To reach different segments of the market."

"Well, what about the independent agents who sell policies for those companies? Shouldn't they offer their clients only the best alternatives?"

"The trouble is, IULs are a little complicated and take some time to explain, Bob. Look how long I've been talking to you and

Becky about them, not counting last week's session. Annuities, on the other hand, are an easy sell. I can explain them in five minutes. And they've been around a long time, so people know what they are. A lot of agents will take the easy way out by making the quick sale rather than doing what's best for their clients. That's the hard truth of it.... Does that answer *that* question?"

"I'm afraid it does.... Okay, let me review some of the things you've said that I want to make sure Becky and I totally understand. First of all, that cap and floor business on the IULs. What you said was that with the cap between fourteen and sixteen percent, I'm going to get some, but not all, of the upside gains in the years when the market goes up more than sixteen percent."

"Right."

"But, because of the floor, I'm never going to suffer any of the losses associated with the market going down below where it was a year before."

"Right again."

"Then I get to reset my starting point every year, and what did or didn't happen the preceding year has nothing to do with gains the following year."

"Correct. If the market is down this year, your floor of zero percent guarantees you against any loss. Then if the market recovers next year, you get all of the gain, up to the cap, added to what you already have, and that gain is then locked in at the end of that policy year."

"What would happen if we didn't have the lock and reset?" Becky asked.

"Oh, brother! You'd be back to doing everything wrong again, Becky. Without the lock and reset every year, your investments could take a beating. For example, I was talking to a woman in the supermarket the other day, and she told me that when the market crashed, two years ago, she lost forty percent of the value of her

401(k), and it's taken her a year and a half just to get back to eighty percent of what she used to have. My clients, on the other hand, sat out the down year without losses or gains, and now, as the market recovers, they're adding to the plus column again. It's harder to recover than to stand still. For example, if you lose thirty percent of your money in one year, you have to earn forty-three percent the following year just to break even."

"Basically, Travis," Bob said, "you're saying I can keep most, but not all, of the market upside and eliminate all of the market downside."

"That's exactly what I'm saying. That's one of the advantages of the Better Money Method."

"Well, I can sure see how it would have a profound effect on my ability to build up a solid nest egg for my retirement. I like the way IULs combine the floor and cap tool with the lock and reset tool."

"Do you see now why some people think IULs are too good to be true?"

"I do, because last week I would have been one of them."

"And you say they've been around for fifteen years, Travis?" Becky asked.

"At least that long."

"Alright," Bob said, "you were going to tell us how the insurance companies can afford to give caps as high as fourteen to sixteen percent."

"Fine. First of all, do both of you fully understand the concept of indexing?"

"I don't understand it at all," Becky said.

"I've read some about it," Bob said. "That's when you invest in a fund that's pegged to an index such as the S&P 500, right? Rather than buying individual stocks."

"That's right."

"In fact, if my memory serves me correctly," Bob added, "I once read in the *Wall Street Journal* that Warren Buffet says indexed funds are the only type of investing anyone should consider if they're going to invest in the market at all."

"Warren Buffet's not the only one to say that. Charles Schwab has said the same thing. And there are others. But let me back up for a minute. Remember when I said that all insurance is basically term insurance that may or may not have something added to it?"

Bob and Becky nodded.

"And I said whole-life insurance pays what they call a 'dividend' of four to five percent."

"Yeah, I'm still with you," Bob said.

"What of it?" Becky asked.

"Well, when universal life insurance started to evolve, some companies decided that, instead of paying a four to five percent dividend, they could take that money and buy an option with it instead."

"What's an option?" Becky asked.

"An option is a contract that gives a buyer the right, but not the obligation, to buy or sell an asset at a specific price on or before a certain date."

"For example, Becky," Bob said, "if we wanted to buy that cute little house we saw last week that was selling for three hundred thousand dollars, but we were a little short of money for the next six months, we could buy an option from the owner for, say, five thousand dollars, to buy the house on or before six months from now. Then, if we found out that the house was worth far more than three hundred thousand dollars, because it was discovered that, say, President Kennedy had slept there one night, the seller would still have to sell it to us for three hundred thousand dollars."

"I get it," Becky said. "And if the seller refused, we would take them to court and have an iron-tight case."

"That's right, honey. And we wouldn't even have to pay any attorney's fees. I would handle it all myself."

"On the other hand, Becky," Travis said, "if you discover that the house, for whatever reason, is worth *less* than three hundred thousand dollars, you can just walk away from the deal, and all you lose is the five thousand."

"I understand that," Becky said. "But what does it all have to do with life insurance?"

"Yeah, Travis," said Bob. "What's the connection?"

"Well, by buying options, insurance companies can increase the return to the policyholders without giving them any of the risk of actually being in the market. So, a company's overall efficiency will determine how much money it has to buy options, and that will determine the size of the cap they offer you."

"Can you explain that efficiency concept a little more?" Becky asked.

"Sure. What all insurance companies do with the money paid into them is similar to what banks do…, only they do it much better."

"Why do you say that?" Bob asked.

"For a few reasons. First of all, they're more closely regulated than banks. Second, they're required to have larger cash reserves than banks. And third, in the last two hundred years or so, not a single insurance company has ever gone broke, assuming it complied with the laws regulating insurance."

"What about AIG?" Becky asked.

"I asked Travis about that, too, honey. It turns out that the insurance wing of AIG was and is doing just fine. It was the mortgage wing that screwed up."

"That's right, Becky," Travis said. "Now, to come back to Bob's question about efficiency. What insurance companies do..., or at least the ones *I* like..., is invest their cash in conservative portfolios until they need the money to pay their overhead and their obligations. Those obligations principally include the death benefits they pay out and the loans that their policyholders may want."

"Wait a second there, Travis," Becky said. "You're telling us that life insurance companies are *obligated* to lend money to their policyholders?"

"Yes, ma'am."

"By law?"

"No, by their own contractual promises."

"Why would they do that?"

"Only the best ones do. And they do it for competitive reasons..., to get your business."

"How exactly does it work?"

"First of all, you don't have to qualify to get the loan, you just have to ask for it. So, if, for example, you were laid off from work, you wouldn't be able to get a loan from a bank, because you wouldn't have income, but you *would* be able to get a loan against your life insurance policy, with no questions asked."

"I like that," Becky said. "So, what kind of terms would there be? For example, if I had a $200,000 policy?"

"Do you mean the policy has a death benefit of $200,000 or a cash value of $200,000?"

"What's the difference?"

"All the difference in the world. The death benefit is what the company will pay out when the policyholder dies. But the cash value is the amount you are earning your interest on. So, if your policy has a cash value of $200,000, and you want to take out a loan of, say, $100,000, your company will give that to you, and charge you anywhere between 0% and 10% interest, depending on how long you've had the policy…, usually between five and ten years.* Let's assume for our example that it is 6%. Now, here comes the best part…. When you take out that $100,000, you continue to earn interest on the cash value of the policy, as if you hadn't taken the money out at all."

"What if I die before I pay it all back?" Bob asked.

"Then the part you didn't pay back will be deducted from the death benefit paid to your heirs."

"What if, instead of dying, I can't pay it back for financial reasons?" Becky asked. "Suppose I still owed $50,000, but couldn't afford to make any more payments. Do I keep paying that 6% interest?"

"Well, let's say your $200,000 cash value is earning 14% annually, because the market is up and you're hitting your cap. That comes to $28,000 in one year. During that same year, you owed 6% on $50,000, which comes to $3,000. That $3,000 is deducted from the $28,000. So, you're still ahead $25,000 in interest, and you haven't paid the $50,000 back. If you were to die that year, that $50,000 would be deducted from the $200,000 death benefit for your heirs."

"What about taxes?" Bob asked. "When Becky gets the $100,000, doesn't she have to pay taxes on it?"

---

*Some companies have a fixed rate between 5% and 6%, whereas others charge you the current Moody's bond rate.

"Not one penny. That's why this method is so amazing. Compare it to what would happen if you tried to do the same thing with a 401(k).... First of all, when you take the $100,000 out of the $200,000 account, you're only going to earn interest on the remaining $100,000..., not the $200,000, as you do with the insurance. Then, if you can't pay off the last $50,000, that amount will be taxed by the federal government and the state as ordinary income..., plus, if you're under fifty-nine and a half when you take out the loan, you'll owe an additional 10% penalty to the federal government."

Becky winced. "Ouch! So, if I can't afford to pay back the last $50,000, the federal and state governments come along and add $15,000 to $20,000 in taxes and penalties."

"Right!" Travis said. "Congratulations! So, is it clear now why IULs are better than 401(k)s?"

"Well," Bob said, "I don't think you finished answering my question about why the life insurance companies you like are so efficient."

"You're right, Bob, I didn't. But you and Becky had some questions that I needed to answer first. Now, to come back to the efficiency issue, the best insurance companies invest the majority of their money in high-quality bonds..., triple A, double A, or triple B.... And they may or may not invest in mortgages on commercial buildings and shopping centers. But if they do, they require a twenty-five to thirty percent down payment to protect themselves. Those portfolios generally average a rate of return of about six percent, and the profit and overhead generally run about two percent. Hence, the approximately four percent rate of return paid on whole-life insurance."

"So," Bob said, "why not just go with whole-life insurance? Why do we need indexed universal life insurance?"

"There are four key reasons. One, IULs cost significantly less. Two, they don't overcharge first and then 'reward' you later with so-called 'dividends.' Three, they are much more flexible. And, four, rather than giving you the four percent rate of return, the way whole-life policies do, IULs instead invest that four percent in options."

"How does that work?" Becky asked. "I know how it works with me buying a house. But how does it work with insurance companies?"

"Well, a company takes that four percent and buys an option based on the performance of an index, such as the S&P 500. That option is what determines the level of the cap on the policies they offer. Their investment can give you a rate of return as high as sixteen percent in some years. Furthermore, because some companies are more efficient than others when managing their overhead, and some companies are content to have lower profit margins than others, those companies will have more money to allocate for options. The more a company has to spend on options, the higher the cap it can offer the policyholder. That's also the reason I prefer companies with a floor of zero over ones that offer a floor of one to two percent, because higher floors raise the costs to the companies, which forces them to offer lower caps."

"I have one question about all this, Travis," Bob said." If I have an IUL with, say, a fourteen percent cap, and the S&P 500 earns twenty percent in a given year, who gets the six percent difference?"

"No one. As I said, the insurance company is taking the money they would normally pay out as a dividend and buying options with it instead. So once they make that purchase, it's out of their hands. If the market goes into the toilet that year, the policy owner gets the floor.... As I said, I prefer a floor of zero because of cost. If the market goes through the roof, then the policy owner gets whatever the cap is. In either event, it is of no consequence to the insurance company. However, I do think they would prefer to have the policy owner make a profit each year, because that makes them look good, which can't hurt."

"You know, Travis," Bob said, "I don't think you've told us the cost of an indexed universal life policy yet, have you?"

"No, and that's a really good question."

"What's your really good answer?" Becky asked.

"Well, as I was telling Bob last week, owning a mutual fund will cost you between $1\frac{1}{2}$ and 2 percent, and owning a 401(k) will cost you over 3 percent. Owning a properly structured IUL, on the other hand, will cost anywhere between 0.6 percent and 2 percent, depending on your age, gender, health, and how you fund it. Folks your age should be close to the 0.6 percent figure."

"Let me get this straight, Travis," Bob said. "With the cap and floor, combined with the lock and reset, I'm guaranteed to never lose any principal. And when the market goes up, I'll get some or all of the gain every year…. My gain at the end of the policy year will be locked in as principal, and then it will be contractually guaranteed against any future loss. Have I got it right?"

"You do indeed."

"I *like* it!"

"I should think so."

"Okay. But just a minute, Travis," Becky said. "I just had a thought…. Since my gain is locked in each year the market goes up, and I have no exposure to the downside, I think I might actually look forward to the market going down in some years. In fact, the more it goes down, the better, because it always comes back up, and when it does, I'll max out my gain on the uptick and really be ahead of the people who are still trying to get back to even!"

"Exactly, Becky. You're not the first one to make that point. On average, the United States has a recession or market correction every eight years. Sometimes they come closer together, and sometimes a little farther apart…. And once they hit bottom, it takes an average of eighteen months for the market to completely recover what it's lost. However, if you choose not to participate in those market corrections, and instead invest in an IUL that has a floor, when the market comes back you will be adding gains to your plus column, while the average investors are still trying to recover their losses."

"You know," Bob said, "what you're saying seems to make all the sense in the world. But, once again, it would really help me if I could see some numbers…, say, from the last ten years or so."

"Well, as it happens, Bob, I have a chart here in my desk that covers the period between 1999 and 2009."

"Did you think he would be unprepared for that question, Bob?" Becky asked. "You should know by now that Travis has an answer for *everything*."

"Thanks for the compliment, Becky…. Now, back in 1999, you two were only teenagers, so you may not have been paying close attention to the stock market."

"I think that's a safe assumption," Bob said.

"Anyway, back in those heady days of the tech boom, everybody was still thinking that the market would go up forever. In fact, if you put $100,000 into an S&P 500 fund in 1999, you would have earned a return on your investment for that year of 19.53%."

"That sounds pretty darn good to me," Becky said.

"It was. But it didn't last. We had downturns in 2000, 2001, and 2002, and then a worse one in 2008…. In fact, that one was the greatest downturn since the Great Depression of the 1930s. So the bottom line is this: at the end of 2009, your $100,000 in the S&P 500 fund would have 'grown' to a little over $89,000."

"You call that *growing?!*" Becky said.

"I was being sarcastic…. Now take a look at the chart. If you put the same $100,000 into an IUL in 1999…, assuming it had a cap of 14% and a 0% floor…, by 2009 your $100,000 would have actually grown to more $195,000."

"Wow!" Bob said. "That's more than a 100% difference…, approximately $90,000 versus more than $195,000!"

"It's even better than that, Bob. As I think I told you the other day, fewer than five percent of all professional money managers match the S&P 500 returns in any one year. So to achieve that $90,000 figure, you would have to outperform 95% of all professional money managers in *every one* of those years.... I think it's fair to say that the chances of you doing that are slim to none."

"Not even Bob is *that* smart," Becky said.

YEAR	S&P 500 INDEX	Zero Floor 14% Cap	$100,000 in S&P in 1999	INDEX BALANCE 0% Floor
1999	19.53%	14.00%	$119,530	$114,000
2000	-10.14%	0.00%	$107,910	$114,000
2001	-13.04%	0.00%	$93,403	$114,000
2002	-23.37%	0.00%	$71,575	$114,000
2003	26.38%	14.00%	$90,457	$129,960
2004	8.99%	8.99%	$98,589	$141,643
2005	3.00%	3.00%	$101,546	$145,892
2006	13.62%	13.62%	$115,377	$165,763
2007	3.53%	3.53%	$119,450	$171,614
2008	-37.00%	0.00%	$75,253	$171,614
2009	23.81%	14.00%	$89,456	$195,640

© Better Money Method
Jensen Cameron

Bob pretended to look hurt.

"Just kidding, honey.... But, Travis, all this raises a question that's been spinning around in my mind for a while."

"Okay, Becky, let's hear it."

"Well, if IULs are as good as you say they are, why doesn't *everybody* own one?"

"Oh, my goodness! Well, I think we might be seeing that happen before you know it. But why doesn't everyone *already* own an IUL? First of all, as I said earlier, the average American has never even heard of them."

"Why do you think that is, Travis?"

"Well, Becky, over the last thirty-five to forty years, a huge industry has been built up around the 401(k)s, the IRAs, and all that.

Those folks have a vested interest in maintaining the status quo, and they spend an awful lot of money doing just that."

"Oh, yeah, I remember," Bob said. "All those Madison Avenue tag lines we talked about last week!"

"Right! And when people tell you they've never heard of IULs, they say it as if that makes IULs bad."

"That reminds me of one of my favorite quotes," Becky said. "'The dumbest people I know,' said Malcolm Forbes, 'are those who know it all.'"

"Very good!" said Travis. "I saw the same idea expressed more scientifically in a book I read some years ago. The author stated that people refuse to accept new paradigms for approximately thirty years..., that's a whole generation. One of the things I found most interesting is that the worst offenders, he said, are the so-called experts, who resist anything in their field that's different from the accepted dogma."*

"I've seen that phenomenon in my own profession," Bob said.

"I'm a schoolteacher," Becky said, "so I've certainly seen my share of that in my profession, too, where the status quo is often king."

"So I hear," Travis said. "Anyway, I think we've finally come to the end of my first pillar, Avoid Market Losses..., unless either of you has any more questions about it."

"I've had enough questions for a while," Becky said. "How about we take you to lunch now at that Italian place?"

"You've got yourself a deal, Becky. From your judgment in restaurants, I can tell you're gonna be making some smart decisions about your retirement investments."

"You're quite a salesman, Travis. Just promise me that, during lunch, we talk about *anything* but money."

---

*Thomas Kuhn, *The Structure of Scientific Revolutions* (Chicago: University of Chicago Press, 1962).

Chapter 6:
Invest Based on Sound Knowledge

"That shrimp fettuccine was wonderful, Travis," Becky said. "You're lucky to have such a good restaurant so nearby."

"I'll resist the temptation, Becky, to say that you're lucky to have such a good investment advisor nearby!"

"I'm glad you resisted," Bob said.

"Alright, are you guys ready to move on to the second pillar of the Better Money Method?"

"Let's see," Becky said, "the first one was Avoid Market Losses. I think we understand that one pretty fully..., don't we, Bob?"

"Sure. So, what's the second one, Travis?"

"The second one is, Invest Based on Sound Knowledge."

"Well," Bob said, "from everything you've told us, and from what I see all around me, most people make their investment decisions for their retirement based on intuition..., or by just following what everyone else is doing."

Travis smiled. "The old lemming syndrome, I call it. Most people find it easier to hope that the myths they hear are reality, rather than taking the time to think for themselves and learn the truth about the subject. So, the first point I want to make this afternoon is that if your money is at risk, you're not investing, you're *gambling*. I don't see any way around that."

"Then, why do most people think you have to take some risk to get a decent rate of return?" Bob asked.

"Well, as I said earlier, there's a huge industry out there with a vested interest in defending the status quo, and they pound into people's heads the notion of 'no pain, no gain.' Aside from that, they can manipulate numbers…, cook the books, as it were. As the old saying goes, 'Statistics never lie, but liars use statistics.'"

"How does that apply to investing?" Becky asked.

"Let me give you an example…. Suppose you have $100,000 to invest, and you buy something that earns you 20% the first year, minus 1% the second year, plus 35% the third year, and minus 40% the fourth year. I could add up those percentages…, which comes to 14…, divide by four…, which comes to 3.5…, and tell you that you had an average return of 3.5%."

"That sounds reasonable," Becky said.

"It does…. And it's even legal for investment advisor representatives like me to recommend some fund to you that had performed exactly like that, and tell you that the fund had an average return of 3.5%…. Now, let's see what you *really* would have if you earned 3.5% per year for four years on $100.000…. Give me a second here with my calculator…. Okay, it comes to $114,752.30."

"Not too bad, Travis," Becky said. "Even if *you* keep the thirty cents."

"Yes, we don't want to forget that thirty cents, do we? That thirty cents is going to pay me to give you my *two* cents on this subject…. Look what happens when an *honest* advisor like me runs the real numbers for you…. If you actually earned those percentages that I named before, year by year, you wouldn't have almost $15,000 more than you started with…, you would have *less* money than you started with."

"No!" Becky said.

"Travis, that's impossible!" Bob agreed.

"Not only possible, guys, but true. In fact, you would have…, at the end of the four years…, $96,228."

"What about the thirty cents?" Becky asked.

"No thirty cents.... So, I ask you…, does that sound like a gain of 3.5% per year?"

"Heck, no!" Bob and Becky said in unison.

"'Heck, no' is about right."

"And you say it's legal for a financial planner to mislead me like that?" Becky asked.

"Unfortunately, honey," Bob said, "it is…, because, technically, it does average out to three and a half percent."

"Even though it doesn't?"

"Not in real dollars."

Travis nodded. "Look at it this way, Becky…. Picture Bob standing in a shower with two shower heads…."

"Oh, I like that!"

"Now imagine that the water coming out of one head is ice cold."

"Ouch!" Bob said.

"And the water coming out of the other head is boiling hot."

"Double ouch!" Bob said.

"I wouldn't want to do *that* to him," Becky said.

"No, you wouldn't. Because even though the *average* temperature of the water falling on Bob might be comfortable, I doubt that he'd want to stand in that shower very long!"

"That's for darn sure," Bob said, mocking what it would be like to boil and freeze at the same time.

© *Better Money Method*
Jemean Cameron

"I can see you've understood everything I've said so far, guys, so let me move on to another point.

"Is it worth thirty cents?" Becky asked.

"You be the judge.... I always advise my clients to give some thought to how much money they will actually need in their retirement, and how long they will need that money to last."

"That's a scary thought, Travis," Bob said. "Most people don't want to think about when they're going to die."

"True enough. But it's an essential part of planning for your retirement. You must make careful calculations about the future. Even bright professional people can look at this business superficially..., and get some rude surprises down the road. For example, I had an engineer in here recently, who was sitting in that chair where you are now, Bob. I don't really know why he came to see me, because he told me, right off the bat, that he wasn't sure he needed any advice. 'My wife and I are set for life,' he said."

"That *is* a little odd, Travis," Bob said. "At my law firm, people never come in just to pass the time of day."

"Well, I was surprised to hear him say he was set for life, and wanted to know why he had come to see me. So, I asked him to tell me a little more about his situation. He said he had a pension of $1,500 a month, and a 401(k) with half a million dollars in it, and he owned his house free and clear."

"That does sound like he was in pretty good shape," said Becky.

"That's what *he* thought, too. So, I asked him how much he needed to live on. 'Well, about $50,000 a year,' he said." Then I asked him what he and his wife got from Social Security, and he said, 'About $1,800 a month.' I did a quick calculation that they were getting $39,600 a year from their pensions and Social Security combined, so I said to him, 'All of your pension is taxable, and a large portion of your Social Security is also taxable, is that right?'"

"Wait a minute," Becky said. "Did you say his Social Security is taxable?"

"It sure is. If your total income is from Social Security, then it's not taxable. But if you have any other income that *is* taxable, you could end up paying taxes on up to 85% of your Social Security income. For example, pension income and income from qualified plans like 401(k)s count as ordinary income, so they can trigger the tax on your Social Security income."

"I didn't know that," Becky said. "I wonder how many people do?"

"I've had people actually argue with me over this, Becky. Or some will say, 'Human Resources never told me that.' Anyway, I told our engineering friend that, to get the $50,000 a year that he said he and his wife needed, he would have to supplement the $39,600 they were getting from the pensions and Social Security with $10,400 from his 401(k). And that was without figuring in taxes and inflation."

"What planet does that happen on, Travis?" Becky asked.

"Mercury in odd years."

"Unfortunately, Mercury is even hotter than Bob's shower!"

"Yes, Becky, you'll come to a speedy retirement on Mercury.... Anyway, I asked the engineer how long he thought his half a million dollars would last. He thought a minute, and then said, 'Taking out roughly $10,000 a year should last us a good fifty years. Since my wife and I are both sixty-five, I don't think we need to worry about that. How many of your clients live to a hundred and fifteen?'"

"He got you there, Travis," Bob said.

"You think so? What the genius engineer didn't take into account..., aside from the taxes and inflation I've already mentioned..., were the medical co-payments he and his wife will be making over the years. I pointed out to him that, if taxes do *not* go up, Uncle Sam would get 25% of his half million..., so there goes $125,000. That leaves $375,000. Furthermore, a 65-year-old couple who have no health issues today are looking forward to paying at least $200,000, in present dollars, for their future medical costs. That leaves $175,000 for him and his wife to supplement the pension and Social Security money..., still not counting inflation.... Then, just to add insult to injury, I pointed out to him that, for a couple aged 65, one of them has a 50% chance of living to 92, and a 25% chance of living to 94."

"What did he say to that?" Becky asked.

"If he was any kind of engineer at all," Bob said, "he could see that $175,000 divided by approximately $10,000 a year, was going to last about seventeen years, which would bring him and his wife about ten years short."

"That's *exactly* what he figured, Bob.... And then he stormed out of my office."

Starting 401K $500,000
Uncle Sam Share −$125,000
Future Medical
Co-payments   −$200,000
                 ─────────
                 $175,000

©Better Money Method

"Sort of like hating the message, so you kill the messenger, isn't it?" Becky said.

"That's what *I* thought. Anyway, that's why I recommend that people take a hard look at how much money they're going to need, and compare that to how much money they're on track to have."

"You may have a serious impact on the suicide rate in this country, Travis," Becky said.

"What I'm really trying to do is encourage people to make a paradigm shift and correct their mistakes before it's too late. There's no point finding all this out when you're ninety."

"That's a fact," Bob said.

"By the way, I don't think I've told you about the *other* millionaire you create with a 401(k) when *you* become a millionaire."

"Now you've gone too far, Travis," Bob said. "What in the world are you talking about? *What* other millionaire?"

"Well, let's assume you start a 401(k) right now."

"Not after what *you've* been telling us!"

"I know, Bob, but just hear me out for a minute. Then I guarantee you'll never give 401(k)s another thought.... So you decide, in your infinite foolishness, to put $8,000 a year into that 401(k), which includes your employer's matching money. Furthermore, the way most people do, you increase that amount every year..., let's say by 3%. Assuming that you're charged fees of 3.7%, which is the national average, the company that administers your 401(k) for you is going to make well over a million dollars off you in fees and interest earned on that money."

"I don't see how that could possibly be true, Travis," Becky said. "That would be outrageous. The American people would never stand for it."

"You're right. They're taking it, lying down.... Take a look at this 'Other Millionaire' table. In fact, you can keep it. After forty years, you've got $1,204,488, and they have $1,209,463."

Becky was astonished. "You mean, they've earned five thousand dollars more than I have on my *own* money?! That's unbelievable, Travis. Are you sure these numbers are accurate?"

"As accurate as any spreadsheet can be."

"But it's all my money, and they make more than a million dollars off me?"

"That's right. It's all in the numbers right there."

"How did you calculate that column called 'Profitable Fees of 2.5%'?" Bob asked.

"Well, if you work for a big company, the average 401(k) costs approximately 3.7%. It's a little higher for smaller companies. I took 1.2% off for accounting, reporting, public relations, and other expenses, leaving 2.5% that I called 'Profitable Fees.'"

"Your assumptions sound reasonable, I have to admit," Bob said. "Now I see how they can spend so much money on those fancy ad campaigns, telling us to come back and invest again each time the market takes us to the cleaners."

You and the Other Millionaire

You	The Other Millionaire
401(k) Contributions of $8,000/Year Increased Each Year by 3%, Earning 7.5%	Your 401(k) Plan Administrator Investing Profitable Fees at the Same 7.5%

Year	401(k) Total Contribution	Starting Value	Investment Return of 7.5%	Ending Value	Profitable Fees of 2.5%	Starting Value	Investment Return of 7.5%	Ending Value
1	$8,000	$8,000	$600	$8,600	$215	$215	$16	$231
2	$8,240	$16,522	$1,029	$17,761	$444	$675	$51	$726
3	$8,487	$25,591	$1,919	$27,510	$688	$1,414	$106	$1,520
4	$8,742	$35,234	$2,643	$37,877	$947	$2,466	$185	$2,651
5	$9,004	$45,479	$3,411	$48, 890	$1,222	$3,874	$291	$4,164
6	$9,274	$56,356	$4,227	$60,582	$1,515	$5,679	$426	$6,105
7	$9,552	$67,893	$5,092	$72,985	$1,825	$7,929	$595	$8,524
8	$9,839	$80,124	$6,009	$86,133	$2,153	$10,677	$801	$11,478
9	$10,134	$93,080	$6,981	$100,061	$2,502	$13,980	$1,048	$15,028
10	$10,438	$106,797	$8,010	$114,807	$2,870	$17,898	$1,342	$19,241
11	$10,751	$121,310	$9,098	$130,409	$3,260	$22,501	$1,688	$24,189
12	$11,074	$136,657	$10,249	$146,907	$3,673	$27,861	$2,090	$29,951
13	$11,406	$152,877	$11,466	$164,343	$4,109	$34,059	$2,554	$36,614
14	$11,748	$170,011	$12,751	$182,761	$4,569	$41,183	$3,089	$44,272
15	$12,101	$188,100	$14,108	$202,208	$5,055	$49,327	$3,700	$53,026
16	$12,464	$207,190	$15,539	$222,729	$5,568	$58,594	$4,395	$62,989
17	$12,838	$227,325	$17,049	$244,375	$6,109	$69,098	$5,182	$74,281
18	$13,223	$248,556	$18,642	$267,198	$6,680	$80,961	$6,072	$87,033
19	$13,619	$270,931	$20,320	$291,250	$7,281	$94,314	$7,074	$101,388
20	$14,028	$294,502	$22,088	$316,590	$7,915	$109,302	$8,198	$117,500
21	$14,449	$319,325	$23,494	$343,274	$8,582	$126,082	$9,456	$135,538
22	$14,882	$345,456	$25,909	$371,365	$9,284	$144,822	$10,862	$155,684
23	$15,329	$372,953	$27,971	$400,925	$10,023	$165,707	$12,428	$178,135
24	$15,789	$401,879	$30,141	$432,020	$10,800	$188,935	$14,170	$203,106
25	$16,262	$432,298	$32,422	$464,720	$11,618	$214,724	$16,104	$230,828
26	$16,750	$464,275	$34,821	$499,096	$12,477	$243,305	$18,248	$261,553
27	$17,253	$497,882	$37,341	$555,223	$13,381	$274,934	$20,620	$295,554
28	$17,770	$533,919	$39,989	$573,180	$14,329	$309,883	$23,241	$333,125
29	$18,303	$570,276	$42,771	$613,046	$15,326	$348,451	$26,134	$374,535
30	$18,853	$609,216	$45,691	$654,907	$16,373	$390,957	$29,322	$420,279
31	$19,418	$650,094	$48,757	$698,851	$17,471	$437,750	$32,831	$470,582
32	$20,001	$692,994	$51,975	$744,696	$18,624	$489,206	$36,690	$525,896
33	$20,601	$738,005	$55,350	$793,356	$19,834	$545,730	$40,930	$586,660
34	$21,219	$785,220	$58,892	$844,112	$21,103	$607,763	$45,582	$653,345
35	$21,855	$834,735	$62,605	$897,340	$22,434	$675,778	$50,683	$726,462
36	$22,511	$886,649	$66,499	$953,148	$23,829	$750,290	$56,272	$806,562
37	$23,186	$941,068	$70,580	$1,011,648	$25,291	$831,853	$62,389	$894,242
38	$23,882	$998,099	$74,857	$1,072,956	$26,821	$921,066	$69,080	$990,467
39	$24,598	$1,057,855	$79,339	$1,137,194	$28,430	$1,018,576	$76,393	$1,094,969
40	$25,336	$1,120,454	$84,034	$1,204,488	$30,112	$1,125,082	$84,381	$1,209,463

NOTE: *Starting in the 35th year, the profitable fees (fees that exceed costs) are larger than the contributions.*

"Travis," Becky said excitedly, "I think I just had an epiphany!"

"Oh, really? What?"

"Well, you said earlier that I could take money out of an IUL any time without taxes or penalties, right?"

"Yes, assuming you've built up some cash value within the policy. For most companies, you'll have to wait at least a year after you've bought the policy."

"And didn't you say that the cost of borrowing against a policy was about two percent in the first ten years, and then zero percent after that?"

"Yes, I did," Travis said.

"Well, then, it seems to me that once I've built up some cash within the IUL, I should use it as my bank to finance big-ticket items like car purchases."

"I was wondering when that light would dawn on you guys. You're one hundred percent correct, Becky. In addition to being able to access emergency cash when you need it, you can also get cash for any other purpose. You just mentioned buying a car. The usual process for that would be to get a loan from the dealer or a bank, and then make payments for five years. By the end of that period, your $25,000 car is worth, maybe, $8,000. And all of your payments for principal and interest have gone to the bank..., never to be seen again. But if, instead, you took a loan from your IUL and then made the payments back to yourself, you would not only avoid paying interest to a bank, but you would also recover all the principal."

"Wow!" said Becky. "That would make a huge difference over a period of time."

"In this case, the difference would be more than $30,000."

"How do you figure that?" Bob asked.

"Alright. In the bank loan scenario, you borrow $25,000 from a bank, and pay that back with interest over five years. At 5% interest, that comes to $28,306.85. Deduct the $8,000 that the car is worth, and you're out of pocket $20,306.85. That's on the one side. On the other side, you take the $25,000 out of your insurance policy, paying the company 2% interest a year, which comes to $1,446.81. At the same time, if you put the identical monthly payments back into your account that you otherwise would have paid to a bank at 5% interest, that adds $28,306.85 to your principal. Deduct the $1,446.81 in interest from that, and you have $26,860.04. In other words, you have $1,860.04 more in your principal than you started with, plus an $8,000 car, for a total in pocket of $9,860.04. When you compare that to the minus $20,306.85 you spent the other way, you're ahead by $30,166.89."

"You figured that out pretty good, Travis," Becky said.

"And the beautiful thing is, unlike a 401(k), the $25,000 you took out of your IUL to buy the car kept earning a rate of return as if the money had never been taken out. If you had taken out a $25,000 loan against your 401(k), the principal in the 401(k) account would be $25,000 less. Over five years, that $25,000, earning 7% interest, is worth $35,440.63. So, there's an additional $10,440.63 for you."

"You're just a cornucopia of cash, aren't you, Travis?" Becky said.

"I try…. And now that you've had one epiphany, Becky, would you like to have another one?"

"Okay, I'm game."

"Let's say you two get married down the road."

"She hasn't even asked me yet, Travis!" Bob said with a big smile.

"Well, after she does…because I can see you two are crazy about each other…there will probably be a child down the road."

"That's a pretty safe assumption, Travis," Becky said. "Probably more than one."

"Okay, let's stay with just one, for the moment. Being the kind of people you are, I'm sure you'll be giving some thought to funding college for him or her."

"Naturally," Bob said.

"That goes without saying," Becky added.

"So, how would you go about it?

"Well, off the top of my head," Bob said, "I guess I would look at one of those 529 plans.... But I suppose you're gonna tell us that you have a better option for that, too."

"How did you guess?"

"Bob's psychic. Didn't you know that, Travis? That's one of the things I love about him."

"In that case, he probably already knows when you're going to propose to him."

"*Touché!*"

"To be serious here for a minute, the idea of getting a 529 plan is not out of line with what most people think. For example, a young couple came to see me about a year ago with their three-month-old daughter on their laps. They couldn't have been prouder of her, and they were also proud of the fact that they had completely funded a 529 plan for her before she was even born."

"They did think ahead, didn't they?" Becky said.

"They sure did. But they had some concerns about the fact that 529 plans, like 401(k)s, are based on market performance. They weren't a hundred percent sure that what they had done would really pay their daughter's expenses by the time she was ready for college. I had to agree that that was a possibility, and it was, of course, too late for them to get rid of the 529 plan. Once you buy it, you own it. Also, they didn't realize that if their daughter did *not* go to college for some reason, they wouldn't be able to access that money until they turned fifty-nine-and-a-half..., unless they wanted to go back to college themselves."

"So, what's the solution?" Bob asked.

"Well, in their case, I sold them an IUL for their own retirement, but there wasn't anything I could do about the college plan. They had already done it before they came to me.... Fortunately for you two, we can set things up the right way from the very beginning."

"What's the right way?" Becky asked.

"Let me tell you what another couple did just recently. They put an IUL on the life of their daughter as soon as she was born. They'll pay $5,000 a year for fifteen years. Then, if and when the girl goes to college, they'll be able to pull out $40,000 a year for four years of college."

"There you go again, Travis," Becky said. "You're a money magician! You're saying that they'll put in $75,000 and take out $160,000?"

"That's right."

"I would do that any day of the week!"

"Me, too," said Bob. "That's a no-brainer."

"It's even better than that," Travis said.

"That's what you always say," Becky taunted.

"And I always have the facts to back it up, don't I?"

"That's why we're listening," Bob said. "How does it get better?"

"Because the money in the IUL..., unlike their house, for example..., doesn't show up on any of their financial statements when their daughter applies for scholarships or financial aid, so the college can't tell the couple to spend that money first. With the house, assuming they had a lot of equity in it, the college would tell them to take some of that out to pay for the kid's college. With the IUL, none of that money needs to be touched. It can stay there and earn interest. And there's one more thing—"

"Hold on there, Travis," Bob said. "Before you get to that, let me explore another possibility with you. What you just said about equity in the house has given me an idea. Wouldn't it make sense, as our child is approaching college age, for us to significantly reduce the equity in our house so that we'd have a better chance of getting financial aid from a college?"

"So long as you put the money in a safe place. You don't just want to fritter it away on cars or travel or other luxuries. And you don't want to have it in the bank, either, where the college can see it as liquid cash. In fact, you don't want it in any account that's considered liquid by the financial aid office."

"What does that leave, I wonder?" Becky said with undisguised irony.

"You got it!" Travis said triumphantly. "The good old IULs."

"As simple as that?" Bob asked.

"There's one precaution. As with any IUL, you can't put in all the money at once..., although, with preplanning, you can arrange to significantly increase your contributions toward the end of the funding period, if you wish."

"Okay, I think I understand all that," Bob said. "Do you, Becky?"

"Sure, we take out a mortgage on our house when our kid's in her senior year of high school."

"Actually, Becky," Travis said, "it would be better to do it in her freshman year of high school, so we can do the preplanning I mentioned."

"Got it!"

"Okay. Now to come back to that one more thing I wanted to mention.... Let's assume that when that couple's daughter graduates from college, she hasn't drained the IUL policy completely, so it's still in force. For her twenty-fifth birthday, after she's been working a few years, her parents give her the policy as a present, and she starts to put $4,000 a year into it, the way other people put money into an IRA. By the time she turns sixty-five, assuming she kept up her contributions all those years, she would have more than three million dollars in her retirement account! That's not a bad return on an investment of $160,000."

"You mean the $160,000 she spent on college?" Becky asked.

"No, the $4,000 times forty years."

"Oh, I see."

"And all through her lifetime," Travis added, "she can use the IUL as her own bank to buy anything she likes…, so long as she pays herself back. I call it the Bank of You."

"The Bank of Becky! I like the sound of that. Especially now that I know it's not too good to be true."

Just then, another sound interrupted the animated conversation—the ringing of Bob's cell phone.

"Hold on a second," Bob said, "I have to take this call from my office. After that, I'll turn the phone off."

"Okay," Travis said, "let's take a ten-minute break."

Chapter 7:
A Helluva Retirement Plan

As Bob took his call, and Travis went through his e-mail, Becky went over to the window to look down at the river, seven stories below. Couples were strolling by the water, children were playing, and a sailboat was just passing by.

"Well," Becky said, when Bob got off the phone, "I'd love to be down with those folks on the river, but we've got more business to transact here with Travis."

"Before we get to pillar number three," Travis said, "I had a thought about something that came up earlier. We were talking about a couple who didn't realize that if their daughter didn't go to college for any reason, the only way they would be able to access the money in their 529 plan would be to wait until they turned fifty-nine-and-a-half or go back to college themselves."

"I remember that," Becky said. "What about it?"

"First of all, if they didn't spend that money on educating their daughter or themselves, they would have to pay taxes on it as they took it out. But if that same couple had put the money in an IUL for their daughter, and she didn't go to college for any reason, they could pull out the money, or any part of it, tax-free, at *any* time they liked, and they could spend it on *anything* they liked, whether it had to do with their daughter or not. They could give the money to their daughter or keep it for themselves."

"I can't imagine keeping my daughter's college fund for myself,"

Becky said.

"Neither can I," said Bob.

"You two are sweet. So, are you ready now to move on to pillar number three?"

"If my brain cells are still working after all the information you've pumped into them," Becky said. "I think number three was Have a Specific Plan for the Next Market Crash..., wasn't it?"

"That's right, Becky, and I don't have that much to say about pillar number three, so your brain cells will get a rest this time around."

"Our brain cells thank you for that, Travis," Bob joked. "It's hard to believe that there are things in this world you don't have much to say about.... Anyway, I already have a specific plan for the next crash. It's the little trick called lock and reset."

"You're an A-plus student, Bob. That's exactly the point. Lock and reset keep you from participating in the next market crash."

Bob smiled. "It's a bit like wearing a foolproof seat belt on the market roller coaster so that you can't fall out when it goes upside down."

"That's a pretty darn good analogy, Bob. I'll have to use it with my other clients."

"But is that all there is to it?" Becky asked, sounding a little disappointed. "We're already finished with the third pillar?"

"I'm afraid so. There's no point in padding what I have to say."

"So the appetizer in this case is the entrée?"

"That's about right."

"Okay," Bob said, "what's pillar number four?"

"Have a Sound Exit Strategy."

"Now, wait a minute there, Travis," Becky said. "You're confusing me. That sounds just like the third pillar."

"They may *sound* the same, Becky, but they're drastically different. While lock and reset are all you need to know to have a specific plan for the next market crash, having a sound exit strategy involves dealing properly with cash flow during your retirement…, not just avoiding the next market crash, which is a whole different can of worms."

"So, the exit strategy you're referring to is from work, not from participating in the market, is that right?" Becky asked.

"Bingo! When most people come to see me, I tell them, 'You've got a helluva retirement plan if you can promise me that you're going to die by age seventy-eight.'"

"That's *mean*, Travis!" Becky said. "How can you say that to people?"

"To wake them up. Should I let them sleep…, and then they wake up broke some day?"

"I guess not."

"Me, either. As I may have said to Bob the other day, the Bureau of Labor Statistics has estimated that only five percent of Americans are able to maintain their lifestyle after they retire. I don't want you guys to be part of the other ninety-five percent. I want you to have enough money in your retirement fund that you always have choice over what you want to do with your lives. In other words, I want you in control of your money, not your money…, or the *lack* of it…, in control of you. That means you need to have a good rate of return on your funds…, and ways to eliminate your taxes."

"You mean *reduce* our taxes, don't you, Travis?" Bob asked.

"No, I mean *eliminate*. I chose the word carefully. I want you to pay *zero* income taxes during your retirement."

"Wow! What a concept!" Becky said. "Zero income taxes. You can really *do* that?"

"I can and have, for myself and my clients. And, with your permission, I'll do it for *you*."

"You must be very popular with the IRS, Travis," Bob said.

"I must admit, I haven't won any popularity contests over there recently."

"Well," Becky said, "I sure can't eliminate taxes with my 401(k). All I can do is delay them."

"That's right," Travis said. "What you're really doing is giving Uncle Sam an IOU to pay him later. He lets you invest your money for forty years or so and take all the risks. Then, when you retire, he tells you how much he wants for himself, and takes it. But if you do things my way, he has to put his hand in someone *else's* pocket."

"How am I gonna waste your tax dollars if you don't pay me any?"

"The only thing my 401(k) administrator talks about," said Becky, "is accumulating assets."

"That's right, Becky. That's their only game. Then they can collect their management fees. The main mantra of all the people pushing 401(k)s is that you need to build a large net worth for your retirement. But they never tell you how you're going to get the money *out* of the 401(k) efficiently, because there's no way to do that as well as you can with an IUL. Basically, they're advising you to build up a huge amount of money inside the account so you can use it up when you retire. The money sits there like a stagnant pond."

"Oh, right!" Bob said. "Uncle Justin told me you were going to make some kind of distinction between ponds of money and something else."

"I sure am, Bob. Let me ask you guys this: How appealing to you are stagnant ponds?"

"Of water?" Bob asked.

"Yeah."

"I must admit," Becky said, "I've never been a big fan of stagnant ponds."

"Ditto," said Bob.

"Right. We all prefer flowing water. And it should be the same thing with money, if you think about it. Ask yourself this: Which do banks prefer, a *pile* of cash or a cash *flow*?"

"How do you mean?" Bob asked.

"Well, when they give you a zero percent credit card, do they tell you not to worry about making any payments for the next six months?"

"Hardly!" Becky said.

"That's right. They give you those cards because they want the stream of cash..., the monthly payments. And that's the same thing *you* should want in your retirement. A stagnant pond of water is the same as that net worth the 401(k) people are always telling you to build. But while they're telling you to do that, do they also tell you about the *death spiral* you'll end up in?"

"Death spiral?!" Becky said, looking shocked. "That's a term you haven't used before, Travis.... What in the world are you talking about?"

"It's my name for the process of taking your money out of one of those stagnant ponds..., in this case, your 401(k)."

"That's a pretty pessimistic way of seeing things, Travis," Becky said. "A *death* spiral for my retirement?"

"Not *yours*, Becky, if *I* have anything to do with it. But I've seen a lot of people go down that spiral over the years."

©Better Money Method
Jenean Cameron

"How does this death spiral of yours work, Travis?" Bob asked.

"Well, it's not mine. I only gave it a name.... Imagine Becky has $500,000 in her 401(k)—"

"I wish!"

"No, you don't, Becky. But imagine it for a minute."

"It feels good to me!"

"It won't, in about three minutes. Now, be serious for a second, Becky. You've got half a million dollars in your 401(k), and forget about Uncle Sam for a minute."

"How in the world do you ever manage to forget about Uncle Sam?" Bob asked.

"You have to learn how to meditate like a yogi," Travis quipped. "Anyway, Uncle Sam can take his cut later. Right now, I want you to imagine that you're retired. You've put your money into laddered

CDs, with different maturity dates, and are earning an average of 3% a year. Let's say you want $50,000 a year to live on. In the first year, you earn $15,000 in interest, and you take out $35,000 to go with that to equal your desired $50,000 income. Now you only have $465,000 earning interest in the CDs, so the second year you earn $13,950 in interest and have to take out $36,050 to equal your $50,000."

"Well, it doesn't take much imagination to see where *this* is going," Becky said.

"No, it sure doesn't. And we haven't even taken inflation into account, let alone taxes. The $50,000 you needed the first year has to grow by 3% for the second year, just to keep up with inflation. In other words, you need $51,500 for the second year. And then $53,045 for the third year..., and so on. At that rate, your half a million dollars will be totally gone in less than ten years."

"Holy mackerel!" Becky said. "Now I see why you call it a helluva retirement plan. It's a great way to go to hell in a handbasket."

"And you'll get there even faster when you bring Uncle Sam back into the picture," Travis said. "He'll cut your ten years down to six or seven."

"Ouch!" said Bob.

"Ouch is for sure!" Becky said. "I have no intention of spending my golden years being a greeter at Walmart."

"And you won't have to, Becky," Travis said, "because an IUL will create a dependable *stream* of cash for your retirement."

"How does it do that?" she asked.

"Well, as you'll recall, you can pull money out at any time without taxes or penalties."

"Yeah, I remember that," Becky said. "But what does that have to do with a stream of cash?"

"As I said earlier, borrowing money from your IUL is like borrowing from a special account that lets you use the money in there as collateral for your loan, and without reducing the interest that collateral is earning. Then, because you have collateral, you get a reduced interest rate on your loan. Let's say you have $100,000 in your IUL, and you want to pull out $20,000. The company might charge you 2% interest on the $20,000, while you're still earning, say, 8% on the $100,000. So, in two years, your principal has grown to $121,306, and you've paid only $1,000 in interest on the loan. Pretty terrific deal, huh?"

"I'll say!" Becky agreed.

"And it gets even better.... If you religiously pay back your loans to yourself with the same interest you would have paid a bank or credit union for that size loan, you'll end up with more money in the account than if you had never taken out the loans at all."

"How can that be?"

"Because the interest you pay to yourself increases the size of your principal..., as opposed to the interest you would have paid to the bank or credit union, which *they* get to keep."

"Okay, that's all terrific, Travis," Becky said. "But, in your example, why would the insurance company charge me 2% interest on my loan and pay me 8% interest on my principal? I don't get that part. It seems to me like a sure way for them to lose money."

"First of all, that 8% number is a reasonable average to expect over time, but it's not what you'll get in any particular year. Some years will be better, some will be worse. There's no guarantees when it comes to the marketplace. I only used it as an example. As for the insurance companies losing money, I wouldn't bet on that. As I said earlier, no American insurance company has gone out of business in the last two hundred years or so."

"Is that really true, Travis?" Bob asked. "None?!"

"None that have complied with the laws. These guys know how to invest money. You could even say that's the primary thing they do.... And that's what they want to do with *your* money..., and Becky's…, and mine…, and the money of millions of other folks. They want to invest your money, and they know that if they offer you an attractive product, you'll buy it. Then they can invest your principal and make a profit off it. It's the same thing banks do, except the insurance companies are required to keep much higher liquid reserves, and they're much more carefully regulated. What I've just described to you, Becky, is called arbitrage."

"Arbitrage? What exactly is that?" Becky asked.

"I can answer that one," Bob chimed in. "An arbitrage, honey, is a transaction that occurs when someone pays interest on money at one rate and earns interest on the same money at a higher rate."

"That's right," Travis said.

Becky still looked confused. "How can you pay interest and earn interest on the same money at the same time? I don't get it."

"Let me give you an example," Travis said. "Let's say you go to the bank to buy a CD, and they give you 3.5% interest on it. Then *I* come in, a little later, and want a second mortgage on my house. Do they give me that loan at the same 3.5% they're paying *you*?"

"No way!" said Becky. "They're probably gonna charge you at least 7% interest."

"Exactly. When they take your money and pay you 3.5% on it, and then loan out your money to me at 7%, that's an arbitrage."

"That's a great deal for the bank," Becky said. "More of an outrage than an arbitrage, if you ask me."

"Not really. Everybody agrees to it every time they make a deposit in their bank."

"But the bank is making 100% profit on *my* money!"

"That's what most people think, Becky. But the truth is, they're earning an *infinite* rate of return, because they don't have any money at all on the table…, zero. It's all someone else's money that they're lending out."

"Okay," Becky said. "I'll live with that one for the moment.

Now let's get back to what that has to do with using an IUL to fund my retirement."

"Well, you can use this arbitrage concept to *your* benefit when you're ready to retire. At that point, you want to pull out a steady stream of cash every year, and you can do that one of two ways…, with what's called a variable loan, or with what's called a zero cost loan."

"What's a variable loan?" Becky asked.

"Okay, I'll explain that first, and then I'll get to the other one…. With a variable loan, you tell the insurance company that you want to earn money on the cash you have in your account, based on what the S&P 500 or some other index does. At the same time, however, you want to pay interest to the company based on some historically lower index, such as the Moody's bond rate. That will allow you to have an average arbitrage on your money throughout your retirement."

"What do you mean by an *average* arbitrage, you old fox?" Becky said.

"Okay, let's suppose you go to your bank and borrow $20,000 at 5% interest for one year, which comes to $1,000. During that year, you lend that money to someone for 15% interest, or $3,000. Your arbitrage for that year would be 10%, or $2,000. For the next year, you continue to pay the 5% interest on $20,000, and lend the money to someone for 9% interest, or $1,800. Your arbitrage for that year is 4%, or $800. Thus, your average arbitrage for the two years is 10% plus 4% divided by two, which comes 7%, or $2,800."

"I understand all that," Becky said.

"Good. Now, with an IUL it's a little more complicated, but works even better for you. In years when the market goes up…, which historically has been about three-fourths of the time…, you will have a positive arbitrage. On the other hand, in the remaining years when the market goes down, you will have a negative arbitrage. But because you have a floor of zero, your negative arbitrage can never be greater than the interest you're paying."

"That *is* more complicated, Travis," Bob said. "Could you illustrate that with dollar numbers, please?"

"Sure. Let's say you have $100,000 in your account, and you borrow that same $20,000 from it that you borrowed from your bank in the other example. You will pay the company, say, 5% interest per year on that loan. Now let's say the S&P 500 goes down 30% that year, which happens from time to time. Since you have a floor of 0%, you can't go lower than that, so your $100,000 neither grows nor shrinks that year. However, you do owe 5% on the $20,000 loan, or $1,000. That $1,000 is entered into the books as money owed to the insurance company, to be deducted from your account if you should die or cancel the policy. Nevertheless, you are still earning interest on the whole $100,000..., not on $99,000, and not on $80,000. In any case, your arbitrage for that year would be minus $1,000 divided by $100,000, or minus 1%."

"Okay," Becky said, "that makes sense..., although I don't like that year."

"Well, it's a helluva lot better than losing 30%, or $30,000, isn't it?"

"I can't argue with that."

"Now," Travis continued, "let's assume that, in the following year, the S&P 500 goes *up* 30%."

"Oh, I like that year much better!" Becky said.

"Me, too!" said Bob.

"Yes, most of us do. Of course, you don't get that whole 30% gain, because you have a cap of, say, 14%."

"Could you make it 15%, please, Travis," Becky said in her sweetest voice.

"Alright, for the sake of the argument..., and because you're so nice..., let's say you have a cap of 15%. At the end of the year, you have $15,000, on top of your $100,000, for a total of $115,000. Since you've kept the whole $20,000 loan, and haven't paid anything back, you now owe $21,000. The 5% interest on that for the following year comes to $1,050. Thus, at the end of two years, you owe the company a total of $2,050. If you were to cancel the policy at that point, you would have $115,000 minus $2,050, leaving you an account balance of $112,950. Thus, for that year, you had a positive arbitrage of $15,000 divided by $100,000, or 15%."

"Sounds good to me," Becky said.

"Yes, so for the two years, you had plus 15% and minus 1%, for a total of 14%, giving you an average arbitrage for those two years of 7%…. Did the old fox answer your question, Becky?"

She smiled.

"Travis, that's truly amazing," Bob said. "In the bank example, starting with the same $100,000, you needed two good years of return to come out in the same place where you came out with the IUL example, in which one year was good and the other was bad. Either way, you averaged 7%."

"That's right. Because the $20,000 that Becky took out of the IUL, in my example, was still *earning* interest, whereas the $20,000 that she borrowed from the bank was *costing* her interest…. Furthermore, I gave her the benefit of the doubt that she lent the money out well, which might not always be the case. But as you noticed, two good years one way didn't do any better, and might easily have done worse, than a good year and a bad year with the IUL scenario."

"Just amazing," Bob repeated. "But I still have another question for you, old fox."

"Shoot, young whippersnapper!"

"When you talked about those interest fees Becky paid on the loan, does she send in monthly checks, or just one at the end of the year, or what?"

"She doesn't send in *any* checks at all, *ever*."

"Never?"

"Never ever."

"So, how do I pay it?" Becky asked. "With gold dust...? Credit cards...?"

"No gold dust or credit cards..., although there *is* a resemblance to credit cards, in that it's just recorded as an entry on a ledger somewhere. Till the day you die..., may it be many years from now..., you will never pay for that loan with cash, check, or any other way. After you die, the insurance company will balance your books, deducting from your death benefit whatever you owe for all the loans you've taken out over the years, and then give your beneficiaries the net death benefit."

"So," Becky said, "if the original $100,000 in my account has grown to, say, $3 million by the time I die, that's my death benefit before the loans and interest are deducted?"

"It may or may not be, depending on how old you are when you die."

"You mean," Bob asked, "the account balance and the death benefit are not the same thing?"

"No, they're not. Not at all. Prior to approximately age 95..., the age varies a little from one company to the next..., the death benefit is always higher than the account balance. After that age, the two amounts are identical. Is that all clear?"

"Yes, it is," Bob said.

Becky nodded.

"Okay, now that you understand variable loans, let me describe how zero cost loans work."

"Oh, Travis!" Becky pleaded. "I've gotta stretch my legs. Can we take a break for ten minutes?"

"Of course, you can."

"Let's go take a walk down the hallway, Bob. I need to cash in one of those kisses Travis said you owe me."

Bob laughed. "Now, there's an offer I can't refuse."

Chapter 8:

Poor on Paper

"You two young'uns stretched out enough yet?" Travis asked.

"We be stretched!" Becky said.

"So, are you ready now to hear about zero cost loans?"

Bob and Becky nodded.

"Alright. Their principal benefit is that they allow you not to take any market risk at all with your loans, if you don't want to."

"What market risk are you talking about, Travis?" Bob asked.

"The one I described a little while back with the S&P 500 versus the Moody's bond rate. Theoretically, there's some risk in that because, although stocks have always outperformed bonds in the long run in this country, past performance, as they say, is no guarantee of future performance. So, if you're allergic to taking *any* risk at all, most companies give you the option of taking out zero cost loans."

"Are they more complicated than variable loans?" Becky asked. "Or less?"

"Oh, less," Travis said.

"Great!"

"Zero cost loans are really quite simple, Becky. Basically, the company pays you a rate of return on your account that is the same percentage as the interest rate you pay on the loans. So, for example, if they pay you 5% interest on your account balance, you pay them 5% interest on your loans."

Bob got excited. "That would guarantee a positive arbitrage, wouldn't it, Travis, since your account balance is always going to be bigger than your loan balance?"

"That's true…, because if you tried to borrow all the money you had in your account, that would collapse your policy."

"Would the company let you do that?" Becky asked.

"They won't let you borrow *more* than your balance, but they will let you borrow right up to your balance, *if* you insist. They'll also warn you first that you're about to do one of the stupidest things in your life, because all the loans you've taken out above your principal will automatically become taxable as ordinary income."

"Well, we're obviously not going down *that* road," Becky said. "Who would ever want to do *that?*"

"There was one 97-year-old guy I heard about who wanted to stick his finger in Uncle Sam's eye. Over a period of a couple of years, he transferred all of his assets out of his name, so that money couldn't be touched. Then he took all the cash out of his IUL. That made him liable for taxes on the several million dollars he had been borrowing from his account over the previous three decades. But when the IRS came after him, he said, 'I'm broke. Go ahead and put a 97-year-old man in jail.' And he got away with it."

"Good for him!" Becky said. "It makes a great story. But I don't think it's going to be *our* story."

"You got *that* right, Becky," Bob said. "But to come back to my question, Travis…. Aside from 97-year-old mavericks, the rest of us are going to borrow less than we have in our account, so that should guarantee a positive arbitrage. For example, to use round numbers, if the insurance company pays me 5% interest on $100,000, or $5,000, that's a lot higher than if I pay the 5% interest on a $20,000 loan, or $1,000."

"Bull's eye, Bob!"

"Then, why wouldn't I just do *that?*" Becky asked. "A guaranteed positive arbitrage sounds good to me."

"It's a matter of temperament, Becky. Some people are happy with a low but steady rate of return, whereas others want some kind of participation in the upside potential of the market."

"Alright, Travis," Bob said, "you've given us a lot of hypothetical examples, comparing 401(k)s and IULs. How about running some real numbers on Becky for us?"

"Is that okay with you, Becky?" Travis asked.

"I can't wait."

"Alright. So, let me see how we should do this.... Let's compare the 401(k) route with the IUL route."

"Okay," Becky said, "go for it."

"Fine.... You're twenty-five, Becky, and you decide to start a 401(k) today."

"Over my dead body!"

"Right. Over your dead body. So, just as in the example with the other millionaire table I showed you earlier, let's say you were lucky enough to earn an average of 7.5%."

"Fat chance of *that* actually happening," Bob said. "I read recently that the average investor only earns about 2.5% on their mutual fund investments."

"Yes, that's true," Travis replied. "But just humor me for a minute, because most folks mistakenly think they're making 7 to 8 percent on their mutual funds in their 401(k)s. It doesn't really matter, anyway, because even with rosy numbers like that, IULs will win the comparison *every* time."

"Bob, give the man enough rope to hang himself with," Becky said.

"I'm planning to hang an IUL policy around *your* neck, Becky," Travis said. "So, let's start with the necklace you *don't* want. Take a look again at that table I gave you with the 'other millionaire' on it. If you funded that 401(k), starting with $8,000 in the first year and then increasing that by 3% each subsequent year, and you were lucky enough to average that 7.5%…, in 40 years, your 401(k), after you deduct fees each year, would be worth…$1,204,488…, and I'll keep the pennies."

"Very nice of you," Becky said. "So long as those pennies don't end up making a millionaire out of *you*."

"No fear of that….Anyway, now you want to start pulling money out of there, and at the same time you want to avoid the death spiral. Most financial planners used to tell you not to pull out more than 3% to 4% a year. But in 2008, all of the standard financial planning models failed. Now studies show that you can't pull out more than about 2.6% if you want a high probability of your retirement money lasting at least thirty years."

"Yes, that's what I've heard," Becky said. "Assuming that the fund grows at 3%, I would be living on the interest, and not touching the principal."

"That would be true if it were not for that other millionaire in there, Becky, taking out her 3.7% every year in fees."

"Oh, yeah, I forgot about her."

"Most people do…. Or rather, most people don't even *know* about her. And those who do, forget about her. The trouble is, *she* doesn't forget about *you*. You can count on her hand being in your pocket, year in and year out."

"We'll have to invite her to Thanksgiving dinner this year, Bob."

"If she'll agree to be the turkey."

"Yeah, that's gonna happen just as soon as Uncle Sam agrees to get his hand out of my *other* pocket."

"Okay, guys," Travis said, "to wrap up the 401(k) scenario, the 3% you take out the first year, Becky, comes to $36,133, before taxes."

"And thanks to your other millionaire," said Becky, "I'll be on the death spiral, as you call it."

©Better Money Method
Juneau Cameron

"First of all, she's not *my* other millionaire, she's *your* other millionaire…, thank you very much. Secondly, as you know, you won't get that $36,133 to keep, but your favorite uncle will be coming around to get his cut. Assuming a tax rate of 25%, that will leave you with…$27,100. If we figure in inflation at 3%, that should be worth, in forty years, about $8,175 in today's money…. But, of course, it'll be even less than that every subsequent year, because your other millionaire pal will be reducing your principal for you every year."

"It sounds like I'll be living in high style, Travis," Becky said.

"Yep, just about high enough to afford that rope you wanna hang me with."

"*Touché!*"

"Okay, now let's take a look at that other necklace…, the one I'm sure you *will* end up buying. In this scenario, Becky, you start putting the $8,000 a year into an IUL, and you increase your annual payments by the same 3% per year for forty years. Let's put those numbers into my software here, and see what comes out…. Okay, at the end of the forty years, you will have paid into the IUL the same amount as you would have put into the 401(k) in the other scenario…, namely, $669,305. After earning interest all those years, and deducting the cost of the insurance, the account would have a cash value of $3,062,969, or approximately $3.1 million."

"That about $1.9 million more than the 401(k)," Bob said.

"That's right," Travis said. "So, which one would *you* choose…, $3.1 million with no taxes, or $1.2 million that gets taxed? Is that a no-brainer, or what?"

"It's mind-boggling, Travis," Becky said, "especially when you realize that most people choose the other way."

"Hopefully, that'll start changing, Becky, as word spreads about this…. Now, let's look at how arbitrage will further compound that $3.1 million for you. As I said earlier, when you want your stream of cash for your retirement, you get to choose between taking out a variable loan every year or a zero cost loan."

"Can I change my mind about that any time I want?" Becky asked.

"With some companies, yes, and with other companies, no. Until recently, once you chose one kind of loan or the other, that was it for the rest of your life. With the companies that don't allow it, the only exception is if you pay off the loan and then take out a new one. But not too many people do that. Most folks make their choice and stay with it. Now, however, more and more companies are allowing you to switch between the two types of loan once a year."

"Do you have a preference yourself?" Bob asked.

"Well, I do have a slight preference for the variable kind. But, as I said, some people prefer to eliminate all risk, and I respect that…. By the way, not all companies offer the variable kind, but all the companies do that I work with…. So, now let's figure out what Becky would get with the variable loan approach, and then we'll figure it out with the zero cost approach…. We said, after forty years, you had $3.1 million sitting in your account."

"That's right," Becky said with a big smile on her face. "I like the sound of that..., \$3.1 million in the Bank of Becky!"

"There you go! So, with the ongoing arbitrage on your \$3.1 million, the numbers that came out of my computer show that you can take out a loan of \$208,448 the first year of your retirement."

"What assumptions are those numbers based on?" Bob asked.

"Great question, Bob. I assumed, first of all, that Becky chose the variable loan option. Then I looked at the default number in the software for what the S&P 500 return has been historically, which is just over 9%. To be on the cautious side, I dialed that down to 8.5%. Then I looked at the default number in the software for what the Moody's bond rate cost has been historically, which is just over 5.7%. To be on the cautious side, I dialed that up to 7.5%. That gave me a positive arbitrage of 1%. Some agents will use a spread as high as 3%, but I think that's totally unrealistic. In fact, anything over 2% is unrealistic in my mind. But I like to be conservative with my clients' money and hope they'll get *more* than I predict. So, using that spread over forty years, and the amounts Becky said she would put in every year..., \$8,000 plus 3%, minus the cost of the insurance, et cetera..., and the number for the first year came out to be \$208,448."

"Okay," Bob said, "I follow you so far."

"And, after that," Travis said, "to keep up with inflation, Becky will increase that amount each and every year by 3%. And all that money will be *tax-free*."

"Let me see," Becky said, looking at her notes. "I'm pretty sure that \$208,448 tax-free is better than \$27,100 after taxes."

"Duh!" Bob said. "More than \$181,000 better.... Almost *eight times* better."

"Wow!" said Becky.

"Octuple wow!" said Bob.

"And that's only for the first year," said Travis. "After that, the

IUL gets better, and the 401(k) gets worse. For most people, the first-year payment from a 401(k) is the *highest* one they're ever going to get…, whereas the first-year payment from an IUL is the *lowest* one they're ever going to get."

"How do you figure that?" Bob asked.

"Because, Bob, I structure them to take account of inflation…, so while the dollar amount goes up, your actual purchasing power stays constant. The 401(k), on the other hand, gets worse because its principal is shrinking every year."

"Well," Becky asked, "isn't the principal in my IUL *also* shrinking, since I'll be taking money out of it every year?"

"No, because of that arbitrage spread that we talked about. Your principal is actually growing by a bigger amount than you'll be taking out in loans."

"I like *that!*" Becky said.

"And here's the kicker: For the 401(k), we assumed a tax rate of 25%. But who says it'll stay there? The chances are it will *increase* down the road."

"Travis," Bob said, "I've gotta ask you a question. You keep talking about taxes going up in the future. Why are you so sure about that?"

"Well, young man, the last time I checked…, which was a while ago, so the numbers are probably worse by now…, the national debt was $74 *trillion*. Trillion with a *t*. That breaks down to approximately $246,000 for every man, woman, and child in this nation. So, whether you're a liberal, conservative, or independent, you're gonna have to pay that bill."

"So what you're saying is that we've been living beyond our means for a long time, and the tab is coming due."

"That's right, Bob. It's no different than if I got ten credit cards in the mail with a $20,000 limit on each one, and then I took off for a trip around the world and charged all the cards to the max. When I

I came back, I would have a problem. As a nation, we hit a wall a long time ago, but we were just too drunk to know it."

That's pretty depressing, Travis," Becky said. "I thought you were going to tell me how great my retirement was going to be."

"Oh, *your* retirement is going to be splendid, Becky. It's just everybody else's I'm worried about."

"Well, let's stay with mine for a minute. I want to hear all those delicious numbers you have for me *after* my first year of retirement. I've got more years than that in me."

"I'm sure you do. So, here are some more tasty numbers for you…. Because of the arbitrage, the bottom line is that the $629,305 you invest over forty years will generate approximately $13 million in tax-free income for you between the ages of sixty-five and one hundred."

"One hundred!" Becky exclaimed. "Travis, you're as generous with the years as you are with the dollars."

"I try…. And if you *do* live that long, you'll still have a death benefit of just under $4 million for your heirs…, and every penny of that will be tax-free."

"I'd better go out and acquire some heirs right quick!" Becky joked.

"On the other hand, Becky," Travis said, "not to be too morbid about it, but the IUL *is* a life insurance policy, after all, so if you die next year, your beneficiaries will get $1,105,638, tax-free. That's not bad for an investment of $8,000…. Especially when you compare it to what your beneficiaries would get if you opened a 401(k)…, namely, the $8,000 you put in, minus taxes and fees."

"All that sounds wonderful," Bob said. "But do your numbers depend on the market performing extremely well?"

"Not at all. If anything, as I said earlier, I based my calculations on highly conservative assumptions…. Remember, a moment ago, when I used 8.5% for the S&P 500 and 7.5% for the Moody's bond rate, with that 1% spread?"

"Sure."

"So, I projected those assumptions that we earlier used for the next forty years all the way out to the next seventy-five years, when Becky turns one hundred."

"What has the stock market averaged over the *last* seventy-five years?" Becky asked.

"I don't have *that* number, but for the last fifty years it's been a little over 10%."

"And how have bonds performed over the years?" Bob asked.

"Well, since 1790, bonds have usually ranged between 4% and 6%."

"So, maybe you've been *too* conservative, Travis," Becky said.

"I would rather err on the side of caution. As the old adage goes, 'Underpromise and overdeliver.'"

"Okay, Travis," Bob said, "have you told us everything you

wanted to about variable loans?"

"That's about it."

"Then, we can move on now to the zero cost loans?" Becky asked.

"We sure can. If you make the same payments to your policy that we used for the variable loan projections, you would have the same amount in your plan at age sixty-five…, that is, roughly $3.1 million. However, during your first year of retirement, instead of getting $208,448, you would get $173,841."

Bob smiled. "That's still more than six times as much as the $27,100 she would get in the first year with the 401(k)," he said.

"So, when I take the loan, Travis," Becky asked, "do I get the money at the *end* of the year…, or the *beginning*…, or *what?*"

"Usually, people ask to get monthly checks…, each one for one-twelfth of the amount they want. They can take more or less than the projected income. In fact, unlike a 401(k), they don't have to take anything at all if they don't want to or need to."

Becky looked fondly at Bob. "If I don't need to take *any* of the money out, I guess someone else will be taking care of me. I wonder who that might be."

"I wonder," Bob said, blushing.

"Do you think you'll still find me attractive, Bob, when I'm a hundred?"

"He'll certainly be attracted to your *money*," Travis said.

"Okay, you two," Bob said, "since you've brought it up, how much *will* she have when she's one hundred if she goes the zero cost route?"

"Well, let's see…," Travis said, looking at a printout. "By increasing her loan by 3% every year, to keep up with inflation, she'll be able to take approximately $10 million out of the account during the thirty-five years between age sixty-five and one hundred."

"That's $2 million less than with the variable loan," Becky said, frowning.

"That's why I prefer the variable," Travis said. "Even with very conservative numbers, it comes out better."

"But you haven't answered my question," Bob said. "How much will the old girl still have when she turns one hundred?"

"Well, with the variable loans, as I said, she'll have a little over $3.8 million."

"And with zero cost loans?" Becky asked.

"With zero cost loans, when you turn one hundred, you'll have $485,945."

"That's not bad," Becky said. "I'll still be *half* a millionaire."

"True, Becky," Travis said, "but you'd better arrange to die *that* year, because when you turn a hundred and one, you'll only have about ninety-two dollars left."

"Ninety-two dollars! How do you like my money now, Bob?"

"I think I'll like it a whole lot better if you go the variable loan route. How much will she have when she turns a hundred and one that way, Travis?"

"Approximately $3.95 million."

"So, her money is still *growing* at that point?"

"Mmm hmm."

"How long will it take her to run out of cash the variable loan way?"

"Forever. In fact, after she turns one hundred, the insurance company stops charging her fees, but she keeps earning her interest, so there's no end to it. If she gets to be a hundred and fifteen, the numbers *really* take off."

"I can't wait," Becky said. "I think that clinches the deal for me toward the variable. Do I have to choose right now?"

"Oh, no. You don't make that decision till you retire. So, you have plenty of time to research it and think about it…. In fact, you have the next forty years. Who else gives you so much time to make up your mind?"

"She *does* like time to make up her mind," Bob said, "so forty years oughta be long enough."

"Very funny," said Becky.

"Yes," Travis said, "you'll have plenty of time to think about it. Of course, during that time, the world will go through a lot of changes, and so will this country and its laws and its economy. But what will stay constant about the Better Money Method is that it will make you rich in cash and assets while you appear poor on paper."

"Oh, right!" said Bob. "You were going to come back to that theme. What exactly do you mean by poor on paper?"

"I mean managing your assets for maximum efficiency. For most people, their biggest asset is their house, right? So, what I recommend is that they periodically…, say, every five years…, pull their equity out of their house, where it's not earning them a penny, and put it into an IUL, where it's liquid, secure, earning interest, and tax-free."

"Hold on there!" Bob said. "You're recommending that I *never* pay off my house!?"

"I suppose I could come up with scenarios in which it worked for you to never pay off your house, Bob. But for most people, that wouldn't be appealing. What I'm really saying is that if you pull that money out of the house from time to time and put it to work for you, rather than just leaving it in the house, in the long run you're going to have a lot more money. And then, if you want, you can pull some of that money out of your IUL and pay off the house with one check."

"You know," Bob said, "as an attorney, I have to admit I can immediately see an advantage to what you're saying, Travis, from the point of view of financial liability."

"How so, Bob?" Becky asked.

"Well, if you and I had a lot of equity in our house —"

"We don't own a house."

"I know…, but we will…, once you get around to proposing to me…. Anyway, if we had a lot of equity in our house, that would be a matter of public record. So if we were ever to get into a major lawsuit and lose, any attorney worth his salt—"

"Or *her* salt!"

"Okay, any attorney worth *her* salt would see that asset and know they had something worth going after."

"I recommend we never get into any major lawsuits," Becky said.

"Nice wish, Becky," Travis cut in, "but that's not totally under your control."

"That's for sure," Bob agreed. "And there's another point, Beck…. If we ever fell behind on our mortgage payments, for some unforeseen financial reason—"

"God forbid!" Becky said.

"I agree…. But if we did, it's unlikely the bank would want to repossess a house with little or no equity in it."

"Right again, Bob," Travis said. "On the other hand, in both of those unfortunate circumstances, if you had your money in an IUL, it would be judgment-proof in most states."

"Assuming all that's true," Becky said. "I still don't understand how it works in practice. How *exactly* do you pull the equity out of your house?"

"Alright," Travis said, grabbing his calculator, "I can show you that. Let's say you buy a house for $400,000, and the bank requires you to put down 20%, or $80,000. You now owe the bank $320,000. Paying 5% interest on the mortgage, with monthly payments of $1,717, after five years, having paid out $103,020, you'll still owe $293,908 on the house."

"Wow!" Bob said. "You're saying that, after five years, we've shelled out more than $100,000, and we've only reduced our debt on the house by about $26,000?!'"

"That's right, Bob. On the other hand, historically, real estate in this country has appreciated by about 6% a year, so—"

"Hang on, Travis!" Bob interrupted. "Not so fast! Six percent appreciation may have been reasonable at one time, but that's not what I've seen recently."

"True, Bob, but I'm talking about the long run here. You can't just look at what's been happening over the past two years. The last fifteen or twenty years give you the big picture."

"Fair enough."

"Let him get on with his example, Bob," Becky said. "I want to hear how we pull our money out of the house."

"Okay, guys, I was saying that your house appreciates at 6% a year. At that rate, after five years, it should be worth..., let me get my calculator again..., $535,000. That is, it's appreciated in value by $135,000. At that point, you take out a loan for 80% of that value of $535,000, which is...$428,000. With that, you pay off the mortgage of approximately $294,000 and keep the difference of approximately $130,000 after expenses. Now, you don't want to just fritter that money away..., you want to invest it wisely and securely. The best place I know to put it is in an IUL. In fact, that will allow you to actually pay off your house faster in the end."

"Really, Travis?" Bob said, looking astonished. "Pay the house off *faster*?!"

"That's right. Without going through all the numbers, you can see at a glance that you're not moving very fast at paying off your house if, after five years, you've spent more than $100,000 and only reduced your mortgage balance by $26,000 or so. If, on the other hand, you took the $130,000 you got from refinancing the house and invested it at 6% annual interest, you would earn $7,800 a year on that. If you then put that against your loan, you can see that you would pay off the house a lot faster. Or, as I said earlier, you can just pay it off later with one check…. And you would do that in the same thirty years you would have paid off the loan the conventional way. Furthermore, after you pay off the house, you'll have more money left over in your IUL."

"Okay, Travis," Becky said, "that part about thirty years from now sounds great. But let's come back to what you said about *five* years from now. I've got $130,000 to put in an IUL. Can I put that whole amount in at once?"

"Excellent question, Becky…. No, at your age, to comply with the tax laws, you would have to put it in over a period of not less than three years and one day. The most efficient way to do that would be to divide the money into four equal payments of $32,500.

"What do I do with the other three payments while I'm waiting?"

"I recommend you put them in laddered CDs so that you're not subject to market risk. Anyway, in our example, you're thirty years old when you refinance the house, so when you're sixty-five, the IUL will have an account value of about $1.2 million. And between the ages of sixty-five and one hundred, you will be able to pull out approximately $5.6 million tax-free. How do like *them* apples?"

"Pretty sweet!" Becky said. "Not a worm in sight."

"Yes, and that's only for your *first* IUL. Every five years or so, you do the same thing…, and before you know it, you're multimillionaires."

"Yeah, Travis," Bob said, looking a little doubtful, "but I still have that nagging thought that the future might not be as rosy as the past. You said that real estate values have gone up about 6% a year in this country, on average…. That's all fine and good. The trouble is, the real estate market, as we've seen, can also go into the toilet. What happens then?"

"Well, if you've taken out your equity and put it into an IUL, you're not hurt by the downturn. And if the downturn comes while you're waiting to take out your equity, you just wait until the market goes up again. In that case, you might have to wait seven or eight or nine years, instead of five."

"What if we need to sell the house for some reason during the downturn?" Becky asked. "For example, if we got jobs in another state?"

"First of all, you haven't pulled out *all* the equity in the house, so you'll still get that back. And you can always borrow from the IUL to make up the difference if you have to sell the house for less than you owe the bank."

"I've thought of another legal reason," Bob said, "for taking the equity out of the house, which you haven't mentioned, Travis."

"What's that? I'm always ready to learn new things."

"If someone, say, fell down the steps in front of my house, and had a mind to sue me, if I didn't have a huge homeowner policy in place, or an umbrella policy, I might be in big trouble. But if I didn't have much equity in the house..., or visible liquid assets of any other kind..., the attorney on the other side would have little incentive to go after me..., or my house."

"Very good, Bob. I'll remember to mention that from now on.... Anyway, that's what I mean by poor on paper. And it doesn't only apply while you're working..., it's just as good after you retire. At that point, your cash and assets will be set up in such a way that they're 100% yours, and 0% Uncle Sam's. You will pay *no* income taxes at all."

"Not even on Social Security?" Bob asked.

"That's right. At least, according to the present ground rules. Right now, your Social Security income can be taxed as ordinary income up to 85%, depending on how much you earn from other sources."

Bob thought about that for a minute. "So," he said finally, "if I have *no* taxable income from other sources, the tax on my Social Security income will be zero, right?"

"There's one current exception, but I'll get to that in a minute. Basically, if you do things my way, the answer to your question is yes. You will be a millionaire in fact, but a pauper on paper. So, you will pay no income taxes of any kind, including on your Social Security."

"What about that exception you mentioned, Travis?" Becky asked.

"Well, a lot of folks like to buy municipal bonds because the income on them is tax-free. The trouble is that, after a certain point, they *do* trigger taxes on your Social Security. It's another form of means testing."

"What exactly is *that?*" Becky asked.

"That's the process whereby the government, in its infinite wisdom, decides you're making too much money, and therefore need to pay an extra tax. That's what they did with Social Security, and they'll probably do it in the future on all other government programs, including Medicare, Medicaid, and everything else."

"You mean, there was a time when Social Security *wasn't* taxed?" Becky asked."

"Sure was. You were born in 1985, right?"

"A lady never tells her age, Travis, except to her doctor...and, I guess, her financial advisor.... So, yes, 1985."

"Alright, about four years before you were born, Ronald Reagan, who was President at the time, and Tip O'Neill, who was the Speaker of the House, created something known as the Greenspan Commission, after its chairman, Alan Greenspan. Well, Greenspan and company decided that the government needed more tax money."

"What a surprise!" Bob said.

"Yes, the nation was shocked to hear it.... Anyway, that's when the government started taxing Social Security up to 85%. My point is, you can get around that with IULs. In fact, IULs are the *only* way you can get around that."

"How does it work, Travis?" Bob asked. "The penalties for tax evasion are pretty stiff in this country, you know. Remember what they did to Al Capone?"

"Don't worry, Bob, I have no intention of sending you or Becky to the big house."

"That *is* one way to get out of paying taxes!" Becky said.

"My way is much more comfortable, Becky. No bars…, unless maybe gold ones…. But, to answer Bob's question about how it works: In addition to choosing between zero cost and variable loans with your IULs, you have two other ways to take your money out after you retire. You can either start by taking out your principal, and then taking loans out on your interest…, or you can take loans out on your interest, and *never* take out your principal."

"Which way is better, Travis?" Bob asked.

"That's an interesting question, because I happen to disagree with most other agents on this point, and I'll show you why…. Most other agents believe that you should start by taking out your principal, and when that's gone, you begin taking out loans on the interest you've earned over the years."

"What's wrong with that?" Becky asked.

"There's nothing wrong with it, except that the other way is better…. If you take out loans on your interest from the very beginning, your principal continues to earn interest. On the other hand, if you start shrinking your principal, the interest on it also shrinks."

"I don't get it," Becky said. "If one way is so clearly better than the other, why do most agents recommend the inferior way?"

"Well, Becky, who knows how these things get started? But once they do, they pick up momentum and are hard to turn around. A lot of us believe in myths without knowing where they came from. There's a story I love to tell that proves the point. A beautiful young bride, who may have looked a lot like you, Becky—"

"Are you an old fox or an old *flirt*?"

"How about a flirty old fox?"

"Okay, but I'm not a bride yet, so don't jump the gun."

"Yeah, Travis," Bob interjected. "Give a guy a little space."

"Alright.... Anyway, that young bride invited her in-laws over for Sunday dinner. After she got the roast ready for the oven, she cut off the end of it and put it in a pan. Watching this, her husband asked, 'Why in the world did you cut off the end?'"

"Yeah, why did she?" Becky asked.

"I'm coming to that.... 'I don't know,' the young woman replied, 'that's always the way my mother cooked a roast.' Well, the next time the young husband was talking to his mother-in-law, he asked, 'By the way, Mom, why do you cut off the end when you cook a roast?'"

"And what did the mother say?" Becky asked. "I'm dying to know."

"Have patience a minute, Becky, and I'll tell you.... The mother-in-law said, 'I don't know, that's the way *my* mother always did it.' So, the husband got on the phone and called Grandma that very minute. 'How come,' he asked, 'you always cut off the end when you cook a roast?' 'Because,' Grandma said, 'my pan was too small for the whole thing.'"

"Oh, that's precious!" said Becky. "I love it!"

"So, you see," Travis concluded, "everybody in the family took that as gospel.... And that's what's happened with those agents I mentioned. In fact, the same dynamic is going on today with IRAs, 401(k)s, 403(b)s, 529 college plans, the whole kit and kaboodle. The point is, just because everybody else is doing it doesn't make it right."

"Speaking about what everybody else is doing, Travis," Becky said, "it's still a gorgeous day out there. How about we take a half-hour break, and Bob and I will go for a walk by the river?"

"That sounds like a great idea," Travis said. "There's a nice little park that runs along the water. It's three blocks up the street to the right when you come out of this building. Plenty of trees and squirrels, if you like that kind of thing.... See you guys in half an hour!"

Chapter 9:
Signing On

"Did you go to the park?" Travis asked.

"We sure did," Becky said, "and we brought you back a Popsicle."

"Thank you kindly.... Strawberry! My favorite flavor. How did you know?"

"Lucky guess," Becky said.

"You know, Travis," Bob said, "that was a funny story you told about the pan. Becky and I were still laughing about it in the park. But then a serious question occurred to us."

"What was that?"

"Well, you used the phrase before, 'according to the present ground rules.' That got us to thinking, what if the government *changes* the ground rules to make IULs illegal? After all, you've pointed out, time and again, how hungry Uncle Sam is to devour our money."

"You know, Bob, life insurance companies are the biggest financial institutions in this country, so I think the chances of the government outlawing life insurance policies are about slim to none."

"But couldn't the government outlaw certain provisions of the policies, such as taking out loans from them?" Bob persisted.

"Unlikely, but it could. Remember how I told you earlier that the IRS didn't like universal life policies and took the matter to the

Supreme Court, which ruled that the policies were perfectly legal?"

"Yes, I remember that," Bob said.

"So, then Congress got into the act by coming up with those laws I mentioned earlier."

"I remember those," Becky said, "because two of them sound like the names of friends of mine, Deborah and Tamara.... Let's see, the names are TEFRA, DEFRA, and TAMRA, right?"*

"Go to the head of the class, Becky. Maybe *you* should go to law school, too."

"Don't give her any ideas, Travis," Bob said.

"Alright.... Anyway, having gone through all that court business and legislation, there's no reason the IRS, Congress, or the courts would want to go through it all again any time soon, I don't think."

"I'll grant you that," Bob said. "Nevertheless, what if the government allows the loans, but makes them taxable?"

"The only way the government could do that is to say that *all* loans are now considered income. So, for example, if you borrowed $25,000 to buy a new car, that would mean you would have to declare that $25,000 as taxable income, even though you're legally required to pay all the money back...with interest."

"That would be even worse than the 'other millionaire' scenario you showed us," Becky said. "I can't believe the American people would hold still for that for one minute."

"Me, either, Becky."

"I'll agree with that, too," said Bob. "So, it's unanimous."

"Even if they drastically change the rules in the future," Travis said, "the government can't undo a legal contract you sign today. That's the *ex post facto* provision of the Constitution we talked about earlier, according to which the government can't undo a contract that was legal at the time it was signed.... And talking about legal

---

*TEFRA: Tax and Fiscal Responsibility Act (1982); DEFRA: Deficit Reduction Act (1984); TAMRA: Technical and Miscellaneous Revenue Act (1988).

matters like that, there's one other thing you should know about IULs, and this should especially interest *you*, Bob. In most states, the money in an IUL is not only exempt from legal judgments, as we discussed earlier, but also from bankruptcy."

"Well," Bob said, "as an attorney, I can tell you that's no minor matter. If a client gets sued and loses the case, he could be wiped out."

"Exactly. But they can't touch the money in your IUL, even if you're thrown into bankruptcy. That makes IULs an especially powerful tool for businesspeople, because if their business goes bust, they can come out the other side with enough liquid cash to start over."

"That's an incredible safety net, Travis," Becky said. "I bet there are a lot of people who wish they knew about *that*."

"It *is* a great selling point, isn't it? And by the way, there's another terrific advantage of IULs for people who own a business. If they anticipate selling it within a few years, they can set up their IUL with that in mind, so they have a protected place to put the money from the sale of their business, and that money can grow tax-free with a nice rate of return in the future."

"That doesn't really apply to us," Bob said, "but I have several clients who are exactly in that position of planning to sell their business down the road, and I'm going to have to tell them about this option. It looks like you'll be getting some more clients before long, Travis."

"Thank you, Bob. Incidentally, planning to sell a business isn't the only way people know in advance that a large chunk of money is coming their way in the future. They may be heirs to a fortune, or they may be selling a tract of land in four to six years, or who knows what, and they want a good place to put that money. So, again, that's where IULs come in."

"At the other extreme," Bob said, "just to wrap up what you

were saying about bankruptcy, it doesn't have to be from business failure..., it can be caused by all kinds of reasons. You could be ruined by medical expenses, by being sued for negligence, and a whole lot of other reasons."

"Absolutely," Travis said. "And in every case, your money in the IUL would be as safe as if it were in a vault in Fort Knox."

"I guess we better get out our pens real quick, Bob," Becky said, "and sign on the dotted line before our dear beloved Uncle Sam thinks up some newfangled ways to grab our money."

"Hang on there, Beck," Bob said. "Let's hear if the old fox has anything more to tell us."

"I do," Travis said. "But I wouldn't be much of a salesman if you were ready to sign, and I kept on jawboning. I can shut up and get out the paperwork if you like."

"No, finish up, Travis," Becky said. "I've got a patient pen."

"Well, the way I see it, IULs will always be better than 401(k)s and other qualified plans, no matter *what* the government does. That means they'll be better for your kids and grandkids, as well as for you. And there are five features of IULs that are unlikely to *ever* be changed, which give them an advantage over all other plans."

"What are those?" Bob asked.

"You've already heard most of them, but let me summarize them for you. First is the lock and reset feature, which protects you from market downturns."

"I like that one," Bob said. "It means we get a higher rate of return."

"It sure does.... Second, you can borrow money from your policy, tax-free, and *never* pay it back."

"I'm sure no other plan does *that*," Becky said with a big smile.

"*I've* never found one," Travis said. "If *you* ever do, let me know about it."

"Fat chance of that," Bob said.

"Right. And that brings me to point number three.... By borrowing against your assets during your retirement, rather than consuming those assets, you don't go into the death spiral, the way you do with the 401(k)s and the other qualified plans, as we discussed earlier."

"Outside of roller coasters in amusement parks," Becky said, "I've never had much interest in taking a ride on a death spiral."

"The only good part about roller coasters," Bob said, "is that she holds on real tight to *me*!"

"I'm sure you can find better ways to get her to do *that*," Travis said.

"We'll discuss that later," Becky said with a blush. "What's the fourth point?"

"Point number four is that IULs cost you less than 401(k)s because the fees on them are much lower. The highest I've ever seen are 2.0%, and the lowest I've ever seen are 0.6%, compared to the 3.7% average for 401(k)s."

"Why is there a range of percentages, and not a fixed one, Travis?" Bob asked.

"The fees depend on a lot of variables, including your age, gender, health, and how you fund the policy. The 401(k) fees are identical for everyone. Does that answer your question?"

"Well," Bob said, thinking about it, "is there 'another millionaire' hidden in the IULs, too? Do the insurance companies make millions off our plan, the way the 401(k) administrators do?"

"The insurance companies do just fine..., you don't have to worry about them, because they know how to invest money. As I said, that's their primary business. The point for you guys to remember is that they charge you much less than the 401(k)s do..., as I said, somewhere between 0.6% and 2.0%, compared to 3.7%."

"That's good enough for me," said Becky.

"That's how I look at it, too," Travis said. "I don't have any quarrel with somebody who's making money, so long as he's making *me* money, too."

"Okay, Travis," said Becky, "you've persuaded us. What's the fifth point?"

"Point number five is that, in addition to all the other benefits, IULs give you a death benefit. No 401(k) does that. As I said earlier, Becky, if you were to put, say, $8,000 into your IUL this year…, and, God forbid, you suddenly die during the year…, your heirs would get $1,105,638, tax-free."

"Yeah, yeah, I remember that. And if I put that same $8,000 into my 401(k) and died during the year, my heirs would get the $8,000, minus taxes and expenses."

"*¡Correctamente!*"

"That's a no-brainer," Bob said. "There's no comparison to which one is better in *that* respect."

"Well, let me ask you this, Travis," Becky said. "Are you saying that I can put $8,000 in an IUL, never put in another penny, live another fifty years, die, and my heirs will get more than $1.1 million?"

"Good try, Becky! No, it doesn't work that way. The insurance companies are too smart for that. The $1.1 million figure was based on the assumption that you were going to make annual payments, just as you've already started to do with your 401(k). If you change that assumption, the results come out totally different. In fact, if you make only one payment, the policy will expire in a year or two and be worth nothing. You won't even get your $8,000 back."

"Well, then, Travis," Bob said, "that seems to me to be the only advantage of a 401(k)."

"How so, Bob?" Travis asked.

"Because if Becky put that $8,000 into a 401(k), and never added another penny, she would still have money in there, whereas the IUL would be worth nothing in a year or two."

"First of all, Bob, that $8,000 in the 401(k) will, over time, earn less money than the fees taken out of it…, as we saw in the 'other millionaire' table…, and it will dwindle away to nothing. Second of all, that scenario will not be relevant to the IUL for very long, after which the policy will *not* expire. So, the only advantage of the 401(k) in this instance would be short-lived and miniscule."

"I agree, Travis," Bob said, "that the scenario I mentioned is highly implausible, but it's technically possible, so I just wanted to hear what your answer would be."

Becky looked a little confused. "But, Travis," she said, "I still don't quite get it. Isn't there life insurance where I can make an $8,000 payment and get a death benefit?"

"Sure, Becky, but that's *term* insurance…. The trouble with that, first of all, is you couldn't get it to cover you for fifty years. And, secondly, there's not a snowball's chance in hell that you'll ever get a term policy for $8,000 that gives you a death benefit anywhere near $1.1 million. At the end of five years, the $8,000 will be gone, and so will the death benefit. In fact, the whole policy will be expired. But that's not what we're doing here. What we're doing is using a form of life insurance to create an investment for your retirement, in the first place, and for your heirs after that. In fact, what I do is set up a policy that is the exact opposite of term insurance. With term insurance, what you want is the maximum death benefit for the least cost. With IULs…, at least, the way *I* structure them…, you get a *living* benefit by minimizing the death benefit and maximizing the amount of cash that can go into the policy."

"But, Travis," Becky said, "I'm sure I'll have kids someday, and at that point I'll want to maximize my death benefit."

"Well, when that time comes, you can always buy a separate term policy."

"Travis," Bob asked, you don't *have* to retire to benefit from an IUL, do you?"

"No, you don't. Good insight there, Bob. You can work right up to your last day on Earth, and take money out of the policy at any age, tax-free."

"*Any* age?" Bob asked.

"*Any* age. Try doing *that* with a 401(k)."

"So, if I want to travel for the last twenty or thirty years of my life," Becky said, "I can do it."

"That's right. Your IUL will give you choice and control over your money and your life."

"And if I want to quit practicing law," Bob said, "and become a sculptor, I can do that."

"You sure can," said Travis. "You can use it for anything you like, including emergencies."

Bob looked very pleased. "If she can have a Bank of Becky," he said, "I guess I can have a Bank of Bob."

"You can have a Bank of Becky, a Bank of Bob, and a Bank of Bob *and* Becky, if you like," Travis proposed.

"So," Becky said, "is it time yet to whip out our pens?"

"In about five minutes," Travis said. "I've got a few more points for you that some people are interested in."

"Like what?" Bob asked.

"Well, there are some riders that can be added to an IUL that can be of great benefit. One is a disability rider. Did you know that, before today's twenty-year-olds turn sixty-five, 80% of them will experience a disability that will keep them out of work for ninety days or more?"

"I guess we both have something to look forward to, don't we, Bob?" Becky said with a wink. "If we're lucky, maybe we can schedule our disabilities to happen at the same time."

"You young folks do an awful lot of thinking about hugging, don't you?" Travis said.

"We try," Bob and Becky said together.

"Now, when you get to be forty," Travis continued, "your chances of having a disability like that go down to 45%..., but that's still a far cry from zero."

"No argument there," Becky said.

"So, with a disability rider, the IUL will pay you money while you're recuperating."

"Is it expensive?" Bob asked.

"Actually, it's quite reasonable. It varies from one company to the next, of course, and by your age."

"Travis," Becky asked, looking serious for a change, "are there any limits on how much disabled time the insurance company will pay for?"

"There's a cap on the amount of money they'll pay out."

"Is that all we need to know about disability riders?" Bob asked.

"That's about it.... Then, there are chronic illness riders. A person is diagnosed as chronically ill *physically* when he can't perform any two out of six normal daily activities. Those include eating, bathing, dressing, toileting, continence, and moving about without assistance. If you're diagnosed as chronically ill *mentally*..., that is, if you have serious cognitive impairment of some kind..., a chronic illness rider will give you the option to receive a portion of your death benefit..., up to 2% a month..., after a waiting period of ninety days."

"We're a little young to be thinking about those kinds of things, I guess," Bob said, "but the reality is that we'll have to think about them sooner or later. Meanwhile, are there any other riders you want to tell us about?"

"Well, if you buy the chronic illness rider, it makes sense to also buy the waiver of charges agreement. That will provide for the payment of monthly charges on your insurance if you become totally and permanently disabled. But it only applies to individuals who are between the ages of 0 and 55. That means that you can buy a policy with this rider for your newborn baby, or you can buy it for yourself, so long as you are under the age of 56."

"That doesn't mean that the payments stop when I turn 56, does it, Travis?" Becky asked.

"Not at all. It just means that you have to be younger than 56 to *buy* a policy with this rider."

"Okay, that's obviously not a problem with either one of us."

"No, and neither of you…, knock on wood…, has a terminal condition, either. But if you should get one down the road, and you want to protect yourself against it with your IUL, the accelerated benefit agreement rider provides for the early payment of a portion of the death benefit. That money is paid out as a loan, and loan interest is charged. The entire amount of the loan is due and payable when you die. This rider can cover such things as care in a nursing home during your final days."

"Let me get this straight," Becky said. "You're saying that if I become disabled, or chronically ill, or am diagnosed with a terminal condition, all I have to do is buy one of these riders, and the company will start paying me money?"

"No way, Becky. You've got to buy the riders when you initiate the policy. If you wait till you're sick or disabled, it's too late…. But good try, again."

"You can't blame me for trying."

"No, I can't. But insurance companies have been around the block for a few centuries, so there aren't too many tricks they don't know…. Let me tell you about one more rider, and we can wrap this up. The guaranteed insurability option agreement rider allows you to buy life insurance in the future without having to take a physical exam all over again, or pass any other requirements."

"Is that it for the riders?" Becky asked.

"Those are the ones my clients have cared about over the years. You can buy all of them, none of them, or any combination. Like IULs as a whole, everything is individually customized to the client."

"With all that customization, Travis," Bob said, "IULs can get pretty complicated. It could take someone *years* to master all this information."

"That's where *I* come in, Bob. I've already spent those years learning about all this, and staying on top of it. As you guys have seen by now, IULs are a great tool…, even though very few people know about them."

"Well," Becky said, "with my big mouth, all my friends and relatives will be hearing about them pronto. So, you better hand me a stack of your business cards."

"Okay, but remember when you're talking to all those folks, not everybody is as open-minded as you. A lot of people are stuck in their old ways, and will fight you tooth and nail on every point."

"Travis, you've covered all the issues Becky and I could think of, and then some," Bob said. "I do believe it's time to sign."

"So," Travis asked, "you're *both* ready to start your first IUL?"

"I have one silly little question about that, Travis," Becky said. "Aside from becoming multimillionaires, the way you described, by our buying a new IUL every five years or so with the money we get from refinancing our house, are there any other benefits from owning more than one IUL?"

"Well, for example, you mentioned having kids, Becky, and wanting to maximize the death benefit. In that case, if your first IUL didn't have a big enough death benefit to meet your needs, you could buy a second one that would increase your death benefit. If that still weren't big enough, we could put a term rider on the new IUL that would increase the death benefit even more for a few years…, say, five or ten."

"Are there any other reasons we might want more than one IUL?" Bob asked.

"Sure. For example, you might earn more money down the road, and want to increase your contributions."

"Then, why couldn't I just increase my contributions into the IUL I already have?" Becky asked.

"You might, depending on how it's structured. But, in general, I've found that it's a lot easier and a lot cheaper to start a new IUL than to modify the original one."

"Why easier?" Becky said. "And why cheaper?"

"The tax laws are set up in such a way that it's easier and cheaper to start a new IUL than to revise an old one. I could go into the details with you about it, but I think your eyes would soon start to glaze over."

"Okay, I'll trust you on that one," Becky said. "So, how many IULs can I have?"

"It depends on your age, your income, your health, and your net worth. One of my clients owns thirty-two."

"Thirty-two?!" Bob said. "Why so many?"

"Well, in his case, he's in poor health, so he can't buy life insurance on himself. Instead, he bought one policy on each of his thirty-two grandchildren. *He* owns the policies, *he* controls all the cash in them, and *he* can give them away or sell them to anyone he wants to."

"Really?" Becky said.

"In theory, yes. Normally, you would expect him to leave the policies to each of the grandkids, but there's nothing to force him to do that."

"Well, I'm ready to sign up for *one* policy," Bob said.

"Me, too!" said Becky.

"Tell you what," said Travis. "Bob, your situation is simple, because you don't have any retirement plans yet. But Becky already has a 401(k) started, so she has to decide what to do with that."

"What are my choices?" Becky asked.

"Well, first off, you could just keep your 401(k), but stop making any more payments into it. Then you could cash it in and pay the taxes on it when you retire."

"What's second off?"

"Second off, you close down the 401(k), pay the penalty and taxes now, and put the remainder into the IUL."

"I must say, Travis, I hate the idea of paying a penalty."

"Most people do. But let me tell you a story about that. I have a client..., we can call him Fred..., who had a 401(k) and bought an IUL, but couldn't bring himself to shut down the 401(k) and pay the taxes and penalty. Then the stock market went through the floor, and the next time I saw him, he said, 'You know, I should have taken your advice and closed out that 401(k). I've lost more money in its depreciation, thanks to the stock market decline, than I would have paid in taxes and penalties.' And by the way, he had that change of heart in less than two months, because when I saw him that second time, he was here to pick up his new IUL policy."

"What do you mean, less than two months, Travis?" Bob asked. "Don't we get our policies within a few days of signing?"

"Actually, Bob, it usually takes between forty-five and sixty days between the time you sign the application for the IUL and the time the company issues the policy."

"Why so long?"

"Well, you have to get a physical exam, you have to be interviewed by the insurance company, and the company has to look over your medical records."

"That should take less than a week."

"Maybe in Japan, Bob, but here things move a little slower. First, you have to schedule a time to be physically examined by a doctor or nurse from the insurance company, and many people put that off for a week or two. Then you have to schedule the interview. Next, your doctor has to send out your medical records, and that's where most of the delays occur. Finally, the underwriter has to find time to review your medical records."

"As Bob said," Becky commented, "that should all take less than a week. It sounds like most of the time is being wasted in-between those steps."

"You're probably right, but that's how it works in most cases."

"We'll do all we can on our end to speed things up," she said.

"Good…. Now, just to finish up with Becky's options for her 401(k), there *is* one more."

Becky smiled. "What's that, old fox?"

"If you really hate the idea of paying taxes and penalties on the plan now, you could roll the money over into an annuity. That would eliminate the market risk, but because the money will be growing over the years in a tax-deferred account, you'll pay taxes on a bigger amount later, and you'll probably be in a higher tax bracket as well."

"It sounds like a no-brainer to me, Travis," Becky said. "The clear winner is to shut down the 401(k), pay the taxes and the penalty, and put the rest of the money into the IUL."

"I couldn't have said it better myself."

"Let's get on with the signing," Bob said. "Becky and I have a reservation for dinner at Chez Chic. I'm looking forward to popping the champagne."

Travis made a few quick entries into his computer and printed out twenty-three pages.

"Okay, Bob, I just have a few quick questions to ask you, and I'll write your answers on these pages."

"Are you going to have me sign over my house to you?"

"Nothing like that. Just things like date of birth, Social Security number, and a few questions about your health. Whether you're a smoker, and that kind of thing."

"Bob's in terrific shape, I can tell you that," Becky said.

"And so is *she*," Bob said.

When Travis had obtained almost all the information he needed, he said, "There *is* one more question, Bob…, the slight matter of who you want as your beneficiary."

Bob shot a nervous look at Becky. "Goodness me, I never thought of that. Pretty crazy, huh, for an attorney? But I haven't given much thought to my own death, to tell you the truth."

"Well, that's perfectly natural for someone your age," Travis said. "But we do need to indicate *somebody*."

Becky put her hand on Bob's. "Honey, why don't you just put your parents in there for now?"

"That's not a bad idea, Bob," Travis said. "You know, you can change your beneficiary anytime you like. When you kids get married, you could make Becky your beneficiary. And when you have children, you can add *them* in."

"And when you get tired of me," Becky joked, "you can take me out of the policy and put in your new girlfriend."

"Very funny," Bob said. "And you can put your new boyfriend in yours."

"We're only kidding, Travis," Becky said. "Bob and I like to be playful with each other."

"Oh, I can see that alright. It's part of what makes you two such a charming couple."

"Okay, enough of that," Bob said. "I'll put down my parents for now. And whenever I'm ready to change it, Travis, what's the procedure?"

"You just have to sign a piece of paper and bring it in here, or mail it, or e-mail a scan, or even fax it. It's as simple as that."

As Bob told Travis the information he needed about his parents, Travis typed it into his computer and then pushed the print button. In no time, Bob was signing his application.

"Now it's your turn," Bob said, "handing the pen to Becky."

Travis printed out Becky's application and handed it to her. She looked down at it, almost fondly, and was just about to sign her name when a thought occurred to her.

"Travis," she said, "I have one last question for you before I sign."

"Okay."

"I'm agreeing here to put $8,000 plus 3% into the policy every year, just as I was planning to do with the 401(k)."

"Correct."

"That's all very well and good..., assuming that my whole life goes smoothly. But things do happen, you know. What if..., I hesitate to ask..., what if something happens to me so that I'm no longer able to keep up those payments? Do I lose the whole thing, like a house being foreclosed?"

"That's a very good question, Becky. It depends entirely on when that unfortunate event occurs. If it's six months from now, there's probably not much I can do for you. If it's a few *years* from now, after you've built up some cash in the policy, and *then* you can't make payments, we tell the insurance company to reduce the death benefit down to a level that's consistent with what you've already put in and that obeys the tax laws.... One caveat about that, though. You better call me and let me know, so I can work it out with the company. Otherwise, you're going to end up paying for a lot more insurance than you need to comply with the tax laws."

"What if I have some good luck and can start making payments again later?"

"That would be one of those situations we discussed earlier, when, depending on the time interval, the best thing to do might be to start up a new IUL."

"What would I do with the old one?"

"You can either just keep it in its reduced form, or you can do what's called a 1035 tax-free exchange and roll the money into the new IUL."

"A 1035 tax-free exchange?" Becky said. "Travis, you *are* a magician! You just pull these concepts out of your hat like a rabbit."

"That's my job."

"I told you we'd be in good hands, Becky," Bob said.

"And without any *slight* of hand, you two. I just tell it like it is.... So, are you ready to sign *now*, Becky?"

"I sure am..., and I'll make *my* parents *my* beneficiaries for now."

"Darn it!" Bob said. "Hold on a sec, Beck. Your question about not being able to make payments the whole time till you're sixty-five raised a question in *my* mind."

"Now, Bob," Becky said, "you're not gonna sabotage this whole thing, are you? After we've spent five hours with this gentleman?"

"No, but..., I can't believe this didn't occur to me earlier.... Travis, Becky's employer has been putting matching funds into her 401(k). I just realized that if she goes with the IUL, she'll lose that, won't she?"

"Not necessarily. I know of a few companies that put matching funds into their employees' IULs.... But you're right, Bob, most don't.... So, Becky, if you wanted to put $8,000 a year into your 401(k), how much of that would come from your employer?"

"My employer matches 25% of my contributions, up to a maximum of $1,000 per year.... So, you're right, Bob. I'll only be able to put $7,000 a year into an IUL, not the $8,000 a year that would go into my 401(k). That *is* something to think about, isn't it?"

"Great question," Travis said. "Most people never ask that. They see the 'free' money from the employer and never get past that point. And all the talking heads reinforce that argument. The trouble is, it's dead wrong. First of all, there's no guarantee your employer will keep its matching fund policy forever. It could decide tomorrow to cancel it. But let's say it does keep it. You're still going to be light years ahead with the IUL. And here's why. Aside from the death benefit, the lower cost, the higher rate of return, the Bank of Becky convenience, and the income being tax-free, you're going to have more dollars in the end."

"How *many* more dollars, Travis?" Bob asked.

"Give me a second to run the numbers.... If we figure that Becky puts in $7,000 a year, and increases that by 3% every year..., at the end of forty years, she will have paid in $550,642, and she'll have an account value of $2,722,879. When she retires, she'll be able to pull out a projected $185,409 her first year."

"What's that worth in today's dollars, Travis?" Becky asked.

"Assuming 3% inflation for the next forty years, that would be equivalent to $55,928 in today's money."

"Well, that's not great," Becky said, "but I guess it's a helluva lot better than the $8,175 I wrote down I would have gotten after taxes with the 401(k)."

"About six times better," Bob said. "But you'll still be pinched."

"And not by *you*," Becky said.

"Don't count on that," Bob retorted.

"You two lovebirds are at it again," said Travis. "But the serious point here is that you really need to figure out what you're going to need in the future to maintain your lifestyle. That's why I recommend that you buy more IULs whenever you can."

"Well, I'm ready to buy my very first one," Becky said. "And I think my pen's ready, too. So, ask your questions, and let's get on with it."

When Becky had given Travis all the information he needed and had signed her application, she and Bob stood up and hugged each other. Then each of them shook hands with Travis.

"I'm so excited about this!" Becky said. "I can't wait to tell my Mom."

"While you're telling her about *your* IUL, Becky," Travis said, "you might suggest to her that she and your dad could buy one, too."

"Aren't they too old to start now?"

"How old are they?"

"Well..., Dad's fifty-three, and Mom's fifty-two."

"They're not too old at all. Not by a long shot. I have many clients who are older than them. In fact, IULs can work for people up to the age of eighty-five."

"Eighty-five?! You're kidding, right?"

"No, I'm not, Becky. The life insurance companies will sell you a policy right up to that age."

"Once again, Travis," Bob said, "I'd like to hear some real-life numbers."

"You know, Bob, ninety percent of my clients are sixty and older. You and Becky are the exception. Very few young people think as far ahead as you guys do. Unfortunately, most people have to reach sixty or sixty-five before they get fed up with their 401k, and all the fees they have to pay on it, and the ups and downs of the market…, not to mention future taxes. And I've found that just about everybody these days is aware of that last point. Sooner or later, usually later, they realize that there hasn't been much growth in their retirement account beyond the money they've been putting in. In fact, when you factor in inflation, you might look like you've been standing still, and actually have less."

"How do you figure that, Travis?" Bob asked.

"Well, you wanted some real numbers, so try these on for size…. Let's say you had $100,000 in your 401(k) in 1999. And let's say you could actually match the performance of the S&P 500 within your 401(k)…, which, of course, for reasons we discussed earlier, you never could…, but *if* you could, at the end of 2010 you would have approximately $102,000."

"Well, at least we broke even," Becky said cheerfully.

"Not really. That's my point, Becky. Because what you've forgotten is that $102,000 in 2010 money is only worth about $70,000 in 1999 money…, thanks to our old friend, inflation."

"Some friend!"

Becky frowned.

"Exactly, Becky. As they say, with friends like that, who needs enemies?"

"Okay, you two," Bob interrupted, "I don't have enough valium to get over this depressing conversation, so let's get back to Travis's hard numbers for investing after you're sixty."

"Well, Bob, I've got four scenarios for you. Let's take case number one. A couple has $400,000 in CDs in the bank, which they don't need for their retirement, but they don't like the low rate of return…, they don't like the fact that, whatever return they get is taxed…, and they're interested in leaving an estate behind for their heirs. What they can do is basically the opposite of what I advocate for you…. That is, they can take the money and make a single lump-sum payment into an IUL, which then becomes a MEC, or Modified Endowment Contract, which we talked about before. But the advantages to them are, one, they're going to get a higher rate of return…, two, they're going to eliminate market loss, which is why they're in the CDs now…, three, they're going to increase their estate…, four, the money will go to their heirs, tax-free…, and five, if they *do* have an emergency and need some of that $400,000, they can still access the original money they put in, without any taxes and without reducing the death benefit."

"How exactly does all that work?" Becky asked.

"Well, suppose you have an emergency of some kind, and need to pull out some of that $400,000…, say, half. If you had a death benefit of $900,000 for your heirs, you could take out the $200,000 to deal with your emergency, and your heirs would still get $900,000…, and tax-free."

"I've gotta agree, Travis," Bob said, "that's a whole lot better than leaving the $400,000 in CDs, earning a miserable one percent, taking out $200,000 for the emergency, and then leaving an estate of $200,000 that the government will take a sizable chunk out of."

"You better believe it…. Ready for case number two?"

"Sure," Bob and Becky both said together.

"Alright. Sometimes I see people similar to ones I just described, but instead of having their money in CDs, they have it in an IRA or 401(k). In that case, when they reach the age of seventy and a half, they're forced to start taking some of the money out every year..., because the government wants to be sure to get its pound of flesh. What that couple can do instead is start taking out that required minimum distribution, and use that money to fund an IUL. By doing that, they can create a tax-free fund that will go to their heirs. Then if they're so inclined, they can leave the residual in the IRA or 401(k) to a charity of their choice. By doing that, the 401(k) serves double duty. The heirs get more than they would have originally, and they get it tax-free..., and the charity gets the remainder of the retirement fund, and that's a tax-deductible contribution, so no taxes are paid on that money."

"Why can't they leave the retirement money to the heirs, too?" Becky asked.

"They can, if they want to. But a lot of people like to leave something to charity without disinheriting their heirs, and this is a good way to do that."

"That's all fine," Bob said. "But our parents don't have that kind of money. What do people do who need to live on their retirement money, and need to make it last as long as possible? In other words, what do *real* people do?"

"That brings me to case number three. With the first two cases, as you have so eloquently noted, Bob, the couples didn't really need the money to live on. They were just trying to be as smart with it as they could. With this third case, the couple has $400,000 in their 401(k), but they need it during their retirement. They want to eliminate market losses, get the best rate of return they can, and avoid all future taxes. What the smart people do in that situation is pull that money out over, say, five years, which would be $80,000 a shot, and put that into an IUL every year. Then, starting in the second year of the IUL, they take out enough money from it to pay the taxes on the previous year's $80,000. They do that every year until they've cleaned out the 401(k) and paid all the taxes on it. Now they have all their money in a tax-free environment, where it will grow and they can withdraw funds tax-free."

"That all sounds pretty good, Travis," Becky said. "But how am I gonna show my mom and dad that they'll be able to maintain their lifestyle while repositioning their money? What about that transition period, when they've got some money in one place, and some in the other?"

"Okay, case number four should demonstrate that. When I'm dealing with people who are in retirement or close to retirement, what I like to do is establish a budget for them that includes a sinking fund."

"What the heck is *that*?" Becky asked. "And please make it simple."

"No problem. A sinking fund is an amount of money you set aside at an assumed interest rate to pay one or more items over a period of time. For example, one of my clients needed $3,000 a month to supplement his Social Security check to maintain his lifestyle for the next six years, until his IUL started to produce cash. We looked at all of his assets, created an account to put his money in, and set aside enough money in that account to fund that $3,000 a month for the next six years. Then we repositioned the balance of his money into an IUL. He was originally worried that his money was going to run out before he did. By repositioning the balance of his money into the IUL, he was able to start pulling out $58,000 a year in the seventh year of the policy…, tax-free. To cope with inflation, the IUL was set up to increase his income by 3% a year, every year for the rest of his life. And since that money is tax-free, it doesn't trigger a tax on his Social Security or any future means testing."

"So, Travis," Bob asked, "does that cover all the bases for old folks?"

"Well, I wouldn't exactly call sixty old, Bob. I used to know what old was, but now I don't anymore. Sixty is the new forty. And that's why people don't want to run out of money. They're living a lot longer these days, and they want to enjoy it.... On the other hand, I've seen folks who ignored my advice and lost their shirts because of the volatility of the market. And the market doesn't need days or weeks to go down anymore. With computers investing, it can go down in seconds, as in that flash crash a while back."

"I saw something about that in the paper," Becky said. "What exactly was that?"

"Well, four or five huge firms have computerized high-frequency trading, based on very thin or narrow arbitrages, so they can make a huge amount of money on a slight variation in the market. And the computers do that much faster than old-fashioned human beings can. What happens in this process is that the computers, in a few milliseconds, spot abnormalities in the market that they can take advantage of and reap great rewards. When the stars line up just right..., or just wrong, actually..., as they did in June 2010, you can get a fifty or sixty percent drop in the market in a couple of minutes. In that case, the drop was so severe that the stock market's computers shut down Wall Street. So the bottom line is, if you've got these huge computerized sales going through, I don't see any way that an average investor can anticipate or correct for flash crashes. And they're only a new headache on top of what's been going on in the market all along."

Becky looked concerned. "What do you mean by that, Travis?"

"Well, if you look at the period between 1929 and 2009, we had eighteen bear markets..., in which the value of stocks fell, on average, at least 15 to 20 percent. Bear markets occur approximately every five years, last about eighteen months, and take around five years to recover from. So you can see from that scenario that people win-lose, win-lose, and win-lose, and that's why they never really get ahead…, other than the contributions they make into the plan."

"Wow!" Becky said. "Now I can see even more clearly the advantages of the zero floor and the lock and reset you talked about as great features of IULs."

"That's one of the reasons, Becky, that IULs appeal to the age group of sixty and over, because one of their primary goals is preservation of capital."

"I understand that," Bob said. "They don't want to run out of money before the game's over. But I have a somewhat different question. When I was talking to my dad about possibly looking into this as an investment for myself, he said, 'That may work for people your age, but for folks my age, it would be too expensive.' What's your response to that, old fox?"

'Well, again, if you're buying life insurance as a death benefit, your dad may be right. But as I've said before, what we're doing with an IUL is buying a *life* benefit, not a *death* benefit. So we're structuring it totally differently from what most people think of when they're buying life insurance."

"Okay, but what about my dad's point about IULs being too expensive at his age?"

"Let me give you a couple of examples."

"Always music to my ears."

"Bob, I recently did a policy on a 63-year-old man who was investing $500,000 in an IUL over a five-year period. When I ran an internal rate of return on his policy, the cost of owning that insurance came out to 1.53 percent. Yesterday, I wrote a similar policy on a 70-year-old man, who just happened to also be investing $500,000 for five years. In his case, the cost of insurance came out to 1.72 percent. So, as you can see, both of these policies actually cost less than owning a mutual fund."

"Why was there a difference in the costs?" Becky asked.

"Age."

"That's it?"

"Age *does* make a difference, even with this kind of policy. But it doesn't drive the cost out of sight, the way everybody believes it does."

"It sounds like you've covered all my dad's objections, Travis," Bob said. "Is there anything else we should know?"

"There *is* one thing.... The best way for people your parents' age to set up IULs is to max-fund them."

"Max-fund?" Becky asked. "Another one of your special terms, eh, Travis? What does it mean?"

"Max-funding means putting in the maximum amount of money in the shortest amount of time that the law allows. I remember one couple who put half a million dollars into an IUL, starting at age 55. They put in $100,000 for each of five years, and then stopped funding the policy. This year, when they turned 65, they started pulling money out. I've calculated that if the wife, who is the policy owner, lives to be one hundred, she and her husband will pull out over four million dollars, tax-free, in the next thirty-five years. Furthermore, if she lives to be a hundred, she'll leave a death benefit for her heirs that is bigger than the original investment of half a million dollars."

"That's a pretty good hunk of change, Travis," Bob said.

"As I mentioned, a *stream* of cash rather than a stagnant pond. That's the key.... And, by the way, max-funding works even better when you're young, because there are more years in front of you for the policy to grow."

"Spell that out a little for us, would you, Travis, please?" Bob asked.

"Sure. I recently had a client..., let's call him Noland..., who's 35 and has set up a plan to put $20,000 a year into his policy for the next thirty years. That comes to a total investment of $600,000. I've calculated that, in thirty years, that policy will have an account value of about $2.1 million. That's pretty good, but it's not max-funding. If he could afford to max-fund the policy, he would put in *half* of that $600,000…, namely, $300,000…, in four annual installments of $75,000…, and in thirty years, his policy would have an account value of about $2.3 million.… $200,000 *more!*"

Bob looked shocked. "You're saying that he could put in fewer dollars now and take out *more* later?!"

"That's *exactly* what I'm saying, Bob. That's the whole beauty of max-funding.… And even the $200,000 difference isn't the whole picture. If that man lives to be one hundred, max-funding his policy will yield one million dollars more in retirement money during the thirty-five years from sixty-five to one hundred, and the death benefit at one hundred will be about half a million dollars higher."

"That's truly amazing!" Bob said. "Just by getting time on his side."

"That and the fact that, under the tax laws, max-funding allows you to reduce the cost of the insurance down to the minimum."

"I just can't wait to tell Mom and Dad about this!" Becky said. "They'll be amazed."

"Okay," Travis said, "but don't be surprised if their first reaction is to say you're crazy, Becky. A lot of folks have trouble adapting to new ideas. They may tell you it's too good to be true."

"They may tell me that, Travis. In fact, I'm sure my dad will use those very words. But I'll just give them your card and let *you* talk some sense into them."

"And I'll be telling *my* parents, too," said Bob. "And all my law partners will be hearing about it as well…, you can count on that, Travis."

"Great. And to soften them up, you might want to show them this table, which summarizes the advantages of IULs over alternative retirement plans. You can each have a copy."

"Can you give me a bunch of these tables, Travis?" Bob asked. "I'd like to pass them out at my office."

"*No problemo.*"

IULs Versus Other Plans

	IULs	Roth Plans	Other Qualified Plans
No stock market risk	X		
Life insurance is included	X		
No contribution limit	X		
Accelerated terminal benefit (up to $1 million from day one)	X		
Loans with no repayment required	X		
Loans can be taken out without restrictions	X		
Policy can be used for "own banker" concept	X		
Earnings can be accessed before age 59$\frac{1}{2}$ with no tax penalty	X		
Minimum distributions are not required at age 70$\frac{1}{2}$	X	X	
Earnings can be accessed tax-free	X	X	
Income is not included in the formula to tax Social Security	X	X	
Net death benefit is left to heirs tax-free	X	X	

"So, what's the next step for *us*?" Becky asked.

"Well, while you're popping that champagne bottle, I'll be ordering the physical exams for you two. An examiner will be calling, and you can schedule the tests for a time and place of your own convenience."

"Can we do it at home?" Becky asked.

"You sure can. The insurance company will order your medical records from the doctors you named on your applications, and then someone from the company will call to interview you on the phone. For the most part, they'll ask you the same questions I asked you today, so be sure to give the same answers. When the policy's approved and shows up at my office, I'll call you, and you'll come down here with your checkbook to sign. After that, you'll have thirty days to change your mind."

"I very much doubt we'll be doing that, Travis," Bob said.

"That's right," Becky said. "It's the best retirement plan I've ever heard of…, even if it didn't have the life insurance part in it."

"That's why I do what I do," Travis said. "And now I guess you two have had enough of this old bird for one day."

"No, you've been great, Travis," Bob said.

"Truly wonderful," Becky added. "Couldn't have asked for more."

"And now," Bob said, "Chez Chic, here we come!"

Chapter 10:
An Unfair Contest — 401(k)s Versus IULs

Ted and Alice Versus Bob and Becky

Back in Chapter 1, when we considered the story of Ted and Alice, there were numerous points in their lives when they had to face less than ideal choices. In every one of those situations, the couple, with their 401(k), were in a worse position than Bob and Becky, with their IULs, would have been in comparable circumstances.

Round 1: The Car Accident

The first crisis that Ted and Alice had to face in their young marriage was the car accident that Alice caused, which, because of insufficient insurance, resulted in a debt of $71,000. To pay that off, which came to almost $80,000 when interest was taken into account, plus making the payments for their new car and the daycare for the kids, Alice had to take a part-time job at Starbucks; Ted had to stop funding his 401(k) for a while, which also cost him the company's matching funds; the couple had to drastically reduce their lifestyle; and Ted had to take out a loan from his credit union, agreeing to make payments for the next five years. Fortunately, thanks to his salary raises at work, Ted was able to pay off the debt in four years.

Had Becky caused that identical accident, instead of Alice, she and Bob would simply have filled out a loan request from their insurance company, asking for the $71,000. Furthermore, they probably would have asked for an even larger sum so that they could buy the new car without having to make monthly payments to a creditor. They would then have repaid those loans to the insurance company over whatever time period was comfortable for them, so as not to deplete the funds in the account. In that way, they would be paying the money back to themselves, unlike Ted and Alice, who handed it over to their credit union, never to see it again. On top of all that, there would have been no question of Bob and Becky having to lower their lifestyle; Becky would not have had to take on additional work; and the couple would have continued to fund their separate IULs.

After Ted and Alice paid off all the debts that emerged as a consequence of the car accident, they decided to make up for the lost time on their 401(k) payments by increasing their contributions to $15,000 a year, which Ted's raises at work made possible. They chose the amount of $15,000 because that was the maximum allowed at the time by law.

On the other hand, as we just saw, Bob and Becky would not have needed to suspend their payments to their IULs, and they would not have been limited by any legal restrictions on the amount they could put into their policies.[*] Furthermore, even though they would have taken money out of their IULs to cover their debts, the principal (or account value) in those policies would not have been affected, so they would still be earning a rate of return on that principal as if they had never taken the loans. That is, they would have been earning a positive arbitrage, paying interest on the loan, but simultaneously earning a rate of return on the account value.

------

[*]Although there is no legal limit to IUL contributions, the insurance companies do impose limits of their own, based on the policyholder's age, gender, income, net worth, and other factors.

174

Round 2: Dad's Heart Attack

The next crisis that Ted and Alice had to face was that Alice's father had a heart attack and needed $15,000 in assistance. To come up with that, Ted reduced his annual contributions to his 401(k) from $15,000 to $10,000 for three years, so he had less in his account than he would have otherwise. In the meantime, he had to take a loan out against his 401(k), since his credit union wasn't lending out money at the time because of the poor economy. That meant that, to generate cash for the loan, Ted had to liquidate some of his mutual fund stock just when the market was significantly down, so the stock was worth less than it had been, and he had to sell more of it than he would have earlier to get the cash he needed. Of course, this reduced the principal in his 401(k). Ted also learned, to his dismay, that if he quit his job or were laid off, he would be required by federal law to repay the loan within ninety days. In addition to that, if he could not repay the loan within ninety days, he would have to pay taxes on the loan as ordinary income and a 10% penalty for an early withdrawal. Fortunately for him, none of that happened, but the thought of it caused Ted and Alice considerable stress.

As with the previous crisis, Bob and Becky would simply have taken a loan from their IULs, with none of the consequences faced by Ted and Alice. They also would have totally avoided the stress of worrying about taxes and penalties, because there would have been none of these, even if they lost their jobs for any reason.

Round 3: The Kids Go to College

When the time arrived for Ted and Alice's children to go to college, the couple had no fund specifically set aside for this cost because of the two previous crises. However, when they applied for financial aid from Jennifer's choice of college, they learned that Ted's income was too high to qualify, and the school regarded their more than half a million dollars in equity in their home as liquid assets, so they were advised to refinance their house. Furthermore, Ted and Alice had to reduce their lifestyle by cutting out dinners, vacations, and other luxuries, and Jennifer (as well as her younger siblings later) had to work part-time and during the summers. The only good news for the couple was that all three kids did not attend college at the same time.

When Bob and Becky's kids went to college, on the other hand, they did qualify for financial aid from the schools, if their parents wanted it, because although the couple had high incomes, they had deliberately kept their equity in their house low, so they didn't show a lot of liquid assets. In other words, although, thanks to their IULs, they had a higher net worth and more liquidity than Ted and Alice, they were "poor on paper." Every five years or so, they had refinanced their house, just as Travis had recommended, so they owned several IULs, including two they had bought at the birth of each daughter as a college fund. Therefore, they didn't really need financial aid if they didn't want it. In fact, after the IULs that Bob and Becky had set up for their daughters paid for the girls' college education in full, they still had an account value of approximately $100,000 apiece! The couple gave those IULs to their daughters as a graduation present, with the advice to use them for their retirement funds. If each girl started putting $4,000 a year into her IUL, instead of an IRA, she would end up with around $3,000,000 in the policy when she got to age sixty-five. Or, by the time she was thirty or so, she could start using the IUL as her own bank—and still have it grow for her retirement.

Round 4: Turning 59$^{1}/_{2}$

When Ted turned 59$^{1}/_{2}$, he was eligible to take money out of his 401(k) without paying a penalty. He was happy about that because by now he had just under $1 million in the account and figured he would invest that in tax-free municipal bonds. However, by this time, federal taxes were 49%, and his state taxes were 11%, so he would have been able to retain only forty cents on the dollar, or roughly $400,000, to invest in the bonds. But none of that happened, in any case, because Ted's company had a policy of not allowing its employees to withdraw any money from their 401(k)s before they retired. To access the money, Ted would have had to quit his job—or wait until he was sixty-five, at which point company policy would have compelled him to retire. Not wanting to wait, and having no desire to quit his job, Ted felt trapped. Fortunately, around this time, the government raised the limits on contributions to 401(k)s, so he started to put in $25,000 every year. Unfortunately, Ted and Alice were certain that, by the time he started pulling money out of his 401(k), federal and state income taxes would be even higher.

Bob and Becky wouldn't have had to worry about any of these things. Certainly, they wouldn't have had any limits on how much money they could put into their IULs. In addition, they wouldn't have had to wait until they were $59^{1}/_{2}$ to access the money in their IULs, because they could do that at any age without paying a penalty—and without ever having to consider quitting their jobs. Furthermore, they didn't have just under $1 million in their IULs, but just under $5.2 million! (And lest anyone forget, Ted and Alice's $1 million was only worth $400,000 after taxes, whereas Bob and Becky's $5.2 million was worth...$5.2 million, after *no* taxes!) By the age of $59^{1}/_{2}$, Bob and Becky each owned four IULs—not counting the two they had given to their daughters. The fact that federal and state income taxes were so high when Bob and Becky were approaching retirement had a much smaller impact on this couple than it did on Ted and Alice, because by keeping a high mortgage, Bob and Becky got a high write-off on their taxes. And they didn't have to worry about income taxes going up after they retired, because at that point they would stop paying any income tax at all!

Round 5: Retirement

When Ted retired at sixty-five, he had just under $2 million in his 401(k). Feeling confident that they were secure, Ted and Alice set off on a longtime dream to tour the country in a motor home. But then, when the stock market plummeted 20%, they aborted their trip, downgraded their lifestyle, and, terrified by the death spiral, Ted went back to part-time work.

The truth is, without knowing it, Ted and Alice were already on the death spiral before they set out on their trip, let alone after the market crashed. That $2 million in Ted's account was an illusion. If he followed Alice's advice, which she had read somewhere, to take out approximately 4% every year to live on, that would mean taking out $80,000 the first year after retirement. But even if they got to keep the whole $80,000, which they didn't, that would represent a significant lowering of lifestyle for the couple. The reason they didn't get to keep all of the money was that their federal and state taxes by this time would take away 65%, or $52,000, leaving them $28,000—which in today's currency would be peanuts.

If Social Security still exists at that time, it might add, after taxes, another $10,000 to their income—if they're lucky. Had Ted and Alice realized this, they would never have set out on their cross-country adventure in the first place. To make ends meet, they would have had to take out far more than 4% a year, or Ted would have had to continue working, or both. Add to all this the stock market crash, which reduced their funds by 20%, and we can see what a mirage that $2 million figure truly was.

When Bob and Becky turned sixty-five, on the other hand, they had a total of $7.8 million in their IULs. Because of the floor on those policies, they weren't hurt at all by the market crash. Then, because of the lock and reset provision, they benefited more than most people when the market rebounded. That is, while 401(k) plans were trying to make up lost ground when the market went back up,

IUL policies were growing. Bob decided to retire from his law firm to become a full-time sculptor, and Becky started a Sheltie Shelter and fussed over her grandchildren.

Round 6: Knockout!

In old age, Ted worked as long as he could. When his health finally forced him to retire, he and Alice took out a reverse mortgage on their house to get by. Ted died at the age of ninety-one. When Alice died, four years later, she had $500,000 left in the 401(k). The federal tax rate was up to 56 percent by then, and the state tax rate was at 18 percent. Since Alice had not set up a trust and transferred her assets into it, her estate had to be probated, which meant that, by law, an attorney got paid 6%. That left 20% for the grieving children: $100,000 divided by three, or roughly $33,000 each. When those children saw how little money their parents had during their declining years, Jenny, Addie, and Teddy were sad and angry beyond belief.

In contrast, Bob and Becky lived in comfort throughout their lives. Five times, they borrowed money from their IULs to buy new cars, and they took several world-class vacations to exotic places around the world. However, in his seventies, Bob developed heart problems, which got him and Becky thinking seriously about the future. Realizing that they had more money than they would ever need, they wanted to find a way to share their life experience, knowledge, and wealth with future generations of their family.

Bob had observed, in his legal practice and elsewhere, that when rich people left a lot of money to their heirs, in more cases than not the money was gone two generations later—if not sooner.

Instead of just leaving money to his heirs, Bob wanted his children, grandchildren, great-grandchildren, and beyond to be hardworking, enterprising individuals with solid ethical principles. In his mind, they should have opportunities available to them, but they should have to earn the right to pursue those opportunities and be responsible for the success or failure of their ventures. Over time, he and Becky developed the concept of what they called the Family Legacy Bank.™

Bob and Becky's Family Legacy Bank

The first thing Bob and Becky had to do was find an attorney who had experience drafting documents for perpetual trusts. Very few attorneys know anything about this, so it took some research to find a good one. Once they found their attorney, they discussed with her what they had in mind, and then she drew up the forms. She also had to draft new wills for them that were compatible with the trust documents.

Next, Bob and Becky had to choose a state that allowed perpetual trusts, since, as their attorney advised them, most states had a limit on the duration of trusts, such as 120 years, after which the money would be dispersed to the heirs with no holds barred. Two of the half-dozen or so states that allowed such trusts especially appealed to Bob and Becky: Alaska and Nevada. They ultimately chose Alaska because it had the oldest law in this area. Their first step in this regard was to transfer some money—in their case, $5,000—to a bank in Alaska that would serve as the trustee of that fund, to comply with the state's laws.

When all the legal formalities were behind them, Bob and Becky called a family meeting, which was attended by their two daughters, Brenna and Bethany, their two sons-in-law, and their five teenaged grandchildren. To make the occasion extra special, they first rented a large beachfront house in Hawaii, so there would be many opportunities for fun.

With everyone gathered around them, Bob and Becky each reviewed their family histories, going back as far as they knew anything about. Their purpose was to give everyone a sense of where they had come from and what values and beliefs had persisted in the two families over the generations. None of this was necessarily new to all but the youngest members of the family, but Bob and Becky wanted to put their own perspective on things. When they finished what they had to say, and after everyone had had a chance to ask questions, Bob and Becky turned to the matter of the Family Legacy Bank.

"Its purpose," Bob said, "is summarized in four words that Grandma Becky and I decided on. Those words are live, learn, give, and earn."

"By live," Becky said, "we mean that we want each of you to follow your own path, whatever that may be, to the fullest. And this bank will be there to enable that."

"By learn," Bob said, "we mean that we want you to grow intellectually and emotionally, and we expect you to share your learning and growth with the rest of us. This bank will enable that, too."

"By give," Becky said, "we mean that we want the bank to make an annual contribution to charitable organizations, to be chosen by the family."

"And by earn," Bob said, "we mean that we want all of you to go out into the world and make an honest living. That doesn't mean that you have to become rich. To the contrary, if you want to do some kind of honorable but underpaid work, the bank might be willing to make up the difference in salary from what you might otherwise earn."

"On the other hand," Becky said, "since we're all a part of the Family Bank, and we all see its benefits, each of you might want to leave your assets to the bank, in order to benefit future generations."

"Grandpa Bob and Grandma Becky," said Brenna's younger son, Burt, "how would this all work in practice? Do we all vote? Is there majority rule? How often do we meet?"

"As long as we're alive," said Becky, "Grandpa Bob and I will appoint a trustee, who will administer the family bank by following the rules established by the trust. Those rules can be modified by the family from time to time, by majority vote."

"Does the trustee have to be a member of the family?" asked Bethany's older daughter, Brittany.

"No, not necessarily," said Bob.

"Does the trustee get paid?" asked Brenna's husband, Ben.

"Yes, a modest amount."

"You didn't tell us how often we meet," said Burt.

"At least once a year," said Becky. "We'll always gather in a new place, and we'll spend part of our time learning about something, but we'll always have plenty of time for fun."

"Can we have some fun right now?" asked Bethany's five-year-old son, "Bug"—and they all headed out to the beach.

After that meeting, Bob lived several more years, until he finally died at the age of eighty-two. Becky lived fourteen years beyond that, so she had the pleasure of watching three great-grandchildren come into the world. When she finally died, at the age of ninety-six, she left no taxes, no probate, and no disgruntled heirs, but more than twenty million dollars in the Family Legacy Bank.™

Getting Started

On June 5, 2010, the *Wall Street Journal*'s News Editor in Personal Finance and Insurance, Leslie Scism, wrote about IULs, "This year's hottest life-insurance product is well-suited to an era of sudden 'flash crashes' and overall uncertainty: It appeals to people eager to capture stock-market gains while avoiding undue risk." However, Scism quotes James Hunt, an actuary with the Consumer Federation of America, as saying about IULs, "One needs a Ph.D. in finance from MIT to completely understand them." While this may be an exaggeration, it is true that there are very few insurance salespeople in this country who fully understand IULs and know how to structure them properly.

If you were given this book by a licensed insurance agent, you should explore with him or her about how an IUL could work for you. If you found this book on your own and need help finding a qualified insurance professional, or if you are an insurance agent or financial professional who would like to learn more about advanced IUL concepts, please contact us at your earliest convenience.

Providence Capital Partners, LLC
dba the Better Money Method™

(425) 818-8256
info@ bettermoneymethod.com
www.bettermoneymethod.com

www.bettermoneymethodbook.com
(to order more copies of this book)